CARYL CHURCHILL

Top Girls

with commentary by
BILL NAISMITH
and notes by
NICK WORRALL

An Open University Set Book
METHUEN DRAMA

The Open University

Methuen Drama Student Edition

10 9 8 7 6 5 4

This edition first published in 1991 by Methuen Drama

Methuen Drama
A & C Black Publishers Ltd
36 Soho Square
London W1D 3QY

www.methuendrama.com

Reissued with a new cover design 1994; with additional material and a new cover design 2005; revised edition 2008; reissued with a new cover design 2009

Top Girls first published in 1982 by Methuen London
Copyright © 1982, 1984, 1990, 1991 by Caryl Churchill
Commentary and Notes copyright © 1991, 2005, 2008 by Methuen Drama

Caryl Churchill has asserted her right under the Copyright, Designs and Patents Act, 1988, to be identified as the author of this play

ISBN 978 1 408 10603 7

A CIP Catalogue record for this book is available from the British Library

Cover Design Jocelyn Lucas
Cover Montage © Jocelyn Lucas 2009

Printed and bound in Great Britain by
CPI Cox & Wyman, Reading, RG1 8EX

Contents

Caryl Churchill

1938	Born in London, 3 September.
1948 –55	Lived in Montreal, Canada.
1957 –60	Read English Language and Literature at Lady Margaret Hall, Oxford. Obtained BA in English.
1958	Student production at Oxford of *Downstairs* (one-act play), also at the *Sunday Times*/National Union of Students Drama Festival in 1959.
1960	Student production of *Having a Wonderful Time* at the Questors Theatre, Ealing.
1961	Student production of *Easy Death* at the Oxford Playhouse. Student sound production of *You've No Need to be Frightened*.
1962	*The Ants* broadcast on the BBC Third Programme.
1967	*Lovesick* broadcast on the BBC Third Programme.
1968	*Identical Twins* broadcast on the BBC Third Programme.
1971	*Abortive* broadcast on the BBC Third Programme. *Not . . . not . . . not . . . not . . . not enough oxygen* broadcast on the BBC Third Programme.
1972	*Schreber's Nervous Illness* broadcast on the BBC Third Programme; lunchtime stage production, King's Head Theatre, London. *The Judge's Wife* televised on BBC TV, directed by James Fermin. *Henry's Past* broadcast on the BBC Third Programme. *Owners*, Royal Court Theatre Upstairs, London, directed by Nicholas Wright.
1973	*Perfect Happiness* broadcast on the BBC Third Programme; lunchtime stage production, Soho Poly, London, directed by Susanna Capon.
1974 –75	Resident dramatist at the Royal Court Theatre, London.
1974	*Turkish Delight* televised on BBC TV, directed by Herbert Wise.
1975	*Objections to Sex and Violence*, Royal Court Theatre, directed by John Tydeman. Sunday night Theatre Upstairs

production of *Moving Clocks Go Slow*, directed by John Ashford.

1976 *Light Shining in Buckinghamshire* with Joint Stock Theatre Group, directed by Max Stafford-Clark, at the Traverse Theatre, Edinburgh, and at the Royal Court Theatre Upstairs. *Vinegar Tom* with Monstrous Regiment, directed by Pam Brighton, at the Humberside Theatre, Hull, and at the ICA, London.

1977 *Traps*, Royal Court Theatre Upstairs, directed by John Ashford.

1978 Contributed with Michelene Wandor and Bryony Lavery to Monstrous Regiment's cabaret, *Floorshow*, at the Theatre Royal, Stratford East. *The After Dinner Joke* televised on BBC TV, directed by Colin Bucksey. *The Legion Hall Bombing* televised on BBC TV, directed by Roland Joffe. (At their request, Caryl Churchill's and Roland Joffe's names were removed from the credits.)

1979 *Cloud Nine* with Joint Stock Theatre Group, directed by Max Stafford-Clark at Dartington College of Arts, Devon, and at the Royal Court Theatre. Revival: Royal Court, September 1980, directed by Max Stafford-Clark and Les Waters. American production: Theatre de Lys, New York, May 1981, directed by Tommy Tune.

1980 *Three More Sleepless Nights*, Soho Poly, London, directed by Les Waters; then at the Theatre Upstairs.

1982 *Crimes* televised on BBC TV, directed by Stuart Burge. *Top Girls*, Royal Court Theatre, directed by Max Strafford-Clark. Transferred to Joseph Papp's Public Theatre, New York. Returned to the Royal Court, February 1983.

1983 *Fen* with Joint Stock Theatre Group, directed by Les Waters, at the University of Essex Theatre, Colchester, and at the Almeida Theatre, London. Transferred to Joseph Papp's Public Theatre, New York, and to the Royal Court Theatre, London.

1984 *Softcops*, Barbican Pit, London, directed by Howard Davies. Contributed with Geraldine Pilgrim, Pete Brooks and John Ashford to *Midday Sun*, at the ICA, London.

1986 *A Mouthful of Birds* with Joint Stock Theatre Group,

written by Caryl Churchill and David Lan, choreographed
by Ian Spink, directed by Ian Spink and Les Waters, at
Birmingham Repertory Theatre, and at the Royal Court
Theatre.

1987 *Serious Money*, Royal Court Theatre, directed by Max
Stafford-Clark. Transferred to Wyndham's Theatre,
London, and to Joseph Papp's Public Theatre, New York.

1988 Contributed to *Fugue, Dance on 4*, choreographed and
directed by Ian Spink, televised on Channel 4.

1989 *Ice Cream*, Royal Court Theatre, directed by Max
Stafford-Clark. Rehearsed reading of *Hot Fudge*, Royal
Court Theatre.

1990 *Mad Forest*, Central School of Speech and Drama,
London, directed by Mark Wing-Davey. Transferred to the
National Theatre of Romania, Bucharest, before opening
at the Royal Court, London.

1991 *Lives of the Great Poisoners*, written for Second Stride
Dance Company, choreographed and directed by Ian
Spink, performed at the Riverside Studios.

1994 *The Skriker*, Royal National Theatre, directed by Les
Waters. *Thyestes* at Manchester and at the Royal Court,
Theatre Upstairs, directed by James Macdonald.

1997 *Hotel*, with music by Orlando Gough, choreographed and
directed by Ian Spink, Second Stride at the Place, London.
This Is a Chair at the Royal Court, directed by Stephen
Daldry. *Blue Heart*, with Out of Joint, directed by Max
Stafford-Clark, at the Traverse Theatre, Edinburgh
Festival, and Royal Court Theatre.

1999 *Blue Heart*, New York and international tour.

2000 *Far Away*, directed by Stephen Daldry, at the Royal Court
Theatre and Albery Theatre.

2002 *A Number*, directed by Stephen Daldry, at the Royal
Court Theatre (winner of the *Evening Standard* Award for
Best New Play).

2004 *A Number*, with New York Theatre Workshop, directed
by James Macdonald.

Synopsis

Act One: Restaurant. Saturday night

Marlene hosts a dinner party in a London restaurant to celebrate her promotion to managing director of 'Top Girls' employment agency. Her five guests are women from the past. In order of arrival they are Isabella Bird (1831–1904), who lived in Edinburgh and travelled abroad extensively between the ages of 40 and 70; Lady Nijo (b1258), Japanese, who was an Emperor's courtesan and later a Buddhist nun who travelled on foot through Japan; Dull Gret, who is the subject of the Brueghel painting *Dulle Griet*, in which a woman in an apron and armour leads a crowd of women charging through hell and fighting the devils; Pope Joan, who, disguised as a man, is thought to have been Pope between 854–856; and, arriving late, Patient Griselda, the obedient wife whose story is told by Chaucer in 'The Clerk's Tale' of *The Canterbury Tales*.

Marlene orders a bottle of wine from the waitress who proceeds to serve the dinner during the scene without speaking at all. On their arrival and throughout the meal the guests recount their individual histories, picking up on each other, interrupting and overlapping. Marlene acts as hostess, ordering courses, drawing out her guests and adding her own comments to the individual stories. This long opening scene, lasting some forty minutes in performance, is one of continuous excited conversation. The orchestration of the dialogue provides climaxes of horror and dismay, humour and celebration. For convenience the lives and stories may be recounted separately, but it is essential to appreciate how the force and energy of the scene is derived from the interconnected structure of the dialogue. It is an extremely challenging scene for practitioners – actors and director – who must find the rhythm in performance to ensure not only that the meal is served and eaten without distracting from the dialogue, but that the guests, however distinctively different, become a chorus communicating more than their individual stories.

Isabella Bird

The daughter of a Church of England clergyman, she moved to live in Scotland. She tried to please her father by conforming to the 'role' of clergyman's daughter, engaging in needlework, music and charitable schemes. She suffered a tumour of the spine and studied poetry, Latin and hymnology. However, she grew to prefer practical things – manual work, cooking, washing, mending, riding horses and a rough open-air life. At forty she was sent to Australia for the good of her health. She found the country hideous, but then she loathed the constant murk and dismal houses of home. She thought her life was over. However, she was greatly cheered and excited travelling from Australia to the Sandwich Islands. She fell in love with the sea. Conditions were awful on board but she felt completely liberated, discovering 'a new world'. She grieved at her father's death, but soon forgot her Latin, and theology made her head ache. She always travelled as a lady and repudiated any suggestion that she was other than feminine. She was admired by a Mr Nugent – Rocky Mountain Jim – who proposed to her because she could both makes scones and lasso cattle. He was, unfortunately, unacceptable as a husband. On her return to England she had a vision of him in his trapper's clothes; it was on the day he died with a bullet in his brain. She had felt a yearning to 'save' Jim Nugent, but the real loves of her life were her sister Hennie and the husband she did marry, Dr John Bishop, who had cared for Hennie during her last fatal illness. She married at fifty, and although Dr Bishop had a 'sweet character' she found married life a drudgery and she fell ill again. When her husband died she determined to leave grief behind and set off for Tibet where, despite suffering from an agonising spine and in face of harsh difficulties, she had great adventures. She always felt dull when stationary. Her memories include being nearly murdered by a howling mob in China, and the little Indian bay mare she rode in the Rocky Mountains. She always suffered guilt on returning to England because she felt her life abroad to be one of self-gratification, so she hurled herself into committee work and wore herself out with good causes. She never left her husband while married but she resented all she had to do in domestic and social work. She declares 'I cannot and will not live the life of a lady . . . Why should I? Why should I?' At seventy she visited Morocco, although very ill, and she was the first European woman ever to see the Emperor. It was only a temporary return of vigour 'but how marvellous while it lasted'.

Lady Nijo

Nijo tells a story of a life of two halves, firstly at Court and later, in obedience to her father's wish, as a vagrant Buddhist nun. 'The first half of my life was all sin and the second all repentance.' At fourteen she was one of the maidens passing the *sake* at Court when the Emperor (aged twenty-nine) told her father to send Nijo to him. He sent her an eight-layered gown which she sent back, not understanding its meaning. She was distressed when the time came, but soon became reconciled to her role – it was what she had been brought up for – and was sad if the Emperor stayed away. She never enjoyed taking other women to him, which was also part of her role. Nijo came from a line of eight generations of poets; her father was a religious man and a poet. He instructed her to 'serve His Majesty, be respectful, if you lose his favour enter holy orders'. When her father died she had only His Majesty and when she fell from favour she had nothing. She adopted religion as a kind of nothing, as if she were dead already. As a nun she travelled the country on foot – she walked every day for twenty years – following the tradition of priests who were often vagrants. Her travels revealed a determined spirit, full of hope and relishing new sights.

One of her lovers was a priest, Ariake. He 'dedicated his life to her' when he came to her and knew he would fall into 'one of three lower realms' when he died. 'Misery in this life and worse in the next, all because of me.' Nijo believed at first that the Emperor was of sweet character because he did not mind about Ariake, but really this was because he no longer cared for her. One night he even sent her to a man who had been pursuing her and listened to their lovemaking from behind the screens. She depended on the Emperor's favour. When she incurred the Empress's displeasure, who claimed that Nijo had no right to wear three-layered gowns, it was explained that she was the adopted daughter of her grandfather, the Prime Minister, and had been granted permission to wear thin silk.

She remembers having some babies, often in embarrassing situations, but she always avoided scandal. Her first child was His Majesty's, which died, and her second was Akebono's. She was seventeen and he had loved her since she was thirteen. He was upset when she had to go to the Emperor, and wrote a lot of poems to her. It was very romantic. When she became pregnant by Akebono she hid the fact from the Emperor. Akebono helped at the birth and took the baby away. It was 'only a girl but I was sorry to lose it'. She saw her daughter once, three

years later; Akebono's wife had adopted the child who was being
brought up to be sent to the palace, as Nijo had been. Her third child
was the son of Ariake the priest, and she never saw the baby after it
was born. Her fourth was also the priest's child, but Ariake died before
the birth and she stayed alone in the hills not wanting to see anyone.
She felt nothing for the child.

Nijo shows considerable interest in Griselda's story, which has many
parallels, and cries at the memory that she did not get her children
back, unlike Griselda. Other painful events in her life were the deaths
of her father and the Emperor. She was not allowed to see the Emperor
when he was dying so she hid in the room with his coffin. Then she
couldn't find her shoes and had to chase the funeral in bare feet,
arriving late, when all that was left was a few wisps of smoke in the
sky. She is deeply anxious and concerned to know whether, if she had
still been allowed at court, she would have been permitted 'to wear full
mourning'.

Nijo remembers an incident that made her particularly angry. She
was eighteen. At the Full Moon Ceremony the men make a special rice
gruel and stir it with their sticks. They then beat their women across the
loins so that they will bear sons, not daughters. The Emperor beat them
hard, which was not exceptional, but on this occasion he allowed the
attendants to beat them too. In response the ladies devised a plan to
attack the Emperor and beat him in return. Nijo beat him with a stick
until he promised he would not order anybody to hit them again. There
was a terrible fuss. The nobles were horrified. That she had beaten the
Emperor with a stick is Nijo's last, exultant, memory.

Dull Gret

Gret makes an early entrance and remains a powerful physical presence
throughout the scene but says little until the end. She is more
preoccupied with the table and the meal than any of the other guests,
being a stranger to sophisticated surroundings. She eats crudely and
steals bottles and plates when no one is looking, putting these in her
large apron. Her rare monosyllabic interjections are coarse, reductive
and amusing and her relative silence adds an element of suspense up to
the point when she delivers her climactic, inspirational story derived
from the surrealistic painting by Brueghel.

She describes coming to hell through a big mouth and finding it – all
black and red – very similar to her own village after it had been fired

and looted by soldiers. Surrounded by devils, including one who showered her and her neighbours with money scooped from his arse, and strange and horrible creatures, she set about beating and fighting these devils. The women were unstoppable. They had known worse than these devils in the form of the Spanish invaders who had slaughtered their families. Gret had lost her eldest son and her baby, killed by soldiers. Finally she could stand no more and shouted to her neighbours 'come on, we're going where the evil comes from and pay the bastards out'. They followed her, in aprons and ordinary clothes, and as they pushed down the street the ground opened up to reveal a big mouth. Gret, waving a sword, led her women, running and fighting, through the mouth into 'a street just like ours but in hell', and gave the devils a beating.

Pope Joan

Joan was an infant prodigy, excited from the age of ten by theology, metaphysics and the teachings of John the Scot. She was always more concerned with knowledge than with active Christianity; she was not a missionary, not concerned to convert. She left home at the age of twelve, dressed as a boy, with a sixteen year old friend. She left because, being female, she was denied access to the library. The two wanted to study in Athens. She went undiscovered and was recognised as very clever. She slept with her friend in a lodging house and nursed him when he fell ill until he died – arguing all the time over the beliefs of famous theologians. She decided to stay a man and devote her life to learning. She went to Rome because Italian men didn't have beards. She studied, obsessed with the pursuit of truth, and taught at the Greek School in Rome. She worked hard and became famous as a speaker when still young. When she was made a Cardinal she fell ill – 'full of terror and regret' – but she recovered and studied in pursuit of the absolute. When Pope Leo died she was elected. She believed she would know God because he would speak to her directly. But He didn't, knowing she was a woman. She eventually took another lover – a chamberlain who was very discreet. She enjoyed being Pope, consecrating bishops and receiving royalty. When there were natural disasters, however, such as earthquakes or plagues, she felt personally responsible. She might have survived happily and successfully were it not for her baby. Here she was finally exposed as a woman and 'Women, children and lunatics can't be Pope'. She hardly knew what was happening during her pregnancy, not being fully conscious of a woman's body, but the chamberlain knew the truth. There was, of course, no question of an abortion and she didn't realise when the baby was due. Her baby was eventually born during the procession of all the Roman clergy on Rogation Day. She experienced labour pains, spasms, contractions and loss of breath. She realised what was happening but couldn't do anything about it. The people thought that she, the Pope, was ill but the baby just slid out on to the road. One Cardinal cried 'The Antichrist!' and fainted. Joan was taken by the feet, dragged out of town, and stoned to death. The baby was also killed. Later the procession always avoided the street journeyed through on the fateful day. The clergy introduced a pierced marble chair in the Chapel of the Saviour to confirm the sex of the Pope. Two clergymen made sure he was a man while the Pope retained his public dignity.

Joan drinks steadily throughout the meal and is quite drunk by the end when she begins to recite Lucretius in Latin before being thoroughly sick.

Griselda
Griselda arrives late and at the most embarrassing possible moment for her. All the guests are drunk and laughing, hugely enjoying the ludicrous idea of the Pope's 'pierced chair', and Gret shouting 'Balls!'. She is diffident, apologetic and orders only cheese and biscuits to eat. Marlene introduces her as famed for an extraordinary marriage recorded by Boccaccio, Petrarch and Chaucer. Her story begins with her marriage.

The daughter of a peasant, Griselda had been spotted for her beauty by the ruling marquis, Walter, when she was fifteen. On the day of his wedding no one knew whom he was to marry, but the procession stopped at her home and he spoke to her father. He had selected Griselda to be his bride. She couldn't refuse, but if she accepted the one condition was that she would always obey him in everything. Ladies dressed her in a white silk dress and put jewels in her hair. At first Walter was kind, but when her first child, a daughter, was six weeks old Walter explained that the people were becoming restless because of her privileged marriage and so he had to remove the child to keep them quiet. She obediently gave up the child, asking only that she be buried where no animals could dig her up. It was Walter's child, to do with as he liked. She never spoke about what had happened and continued to live happily with Walter. After four years she had a son, and two years later Walter again said that the people were angry that their heir was a peasant's grandson. Griselda believed that when he took her children it was to test her love for him, but 'it was always easy because I always knew I would do what he said'. Twelve years later she was tested again. Walter decided he must marry someone who could give him an acceptable heir. Griselda was sent home, barefoot and dressed only in a slip. Her father and everyone else were crying but she was perfectly content. Quite soon afterwards she was sent for again, to prepare his wedding to a young girl from France – a beautiful girl of sixteen who had her younger brother with her as a page. The guests entered for the feast but Walter stayed behind and put his arms around Griselda and kissed her. She felt half asleep with shock, and he said 'this is your daughter and your son'. Griselda fainted, then cried and kissed her children. She was dressed in a cloth of gold and lived happily with Walter who had 'suffered so much all those years'.

The guests react with amazement at Griselda's remarkable story but Marlene follows it with a particularly scathing commentary on Walter. Eventually, following Nijo's story of the attack on the Emperor, even Griselda begins to re-think – 'I do think – I do wonder – it would have been nicer if Walter hadn't had to'.

Act Two, Scene One: 'Top Girls' Employment Agency – Monday morning

In the 'Top Girls' Employment Agency Marlene interviews Jeanine and quickly establishes the relevant details concerning her career. She has six 'O' level passes and moderate secretarial skills. She could have continued her formal education but preferred to go to work. She started as a typist in a small friendly office where she has progressed to being a secretary, shared by three executives. She earns £100 a week, which Marlene considers 'not bad', but she feels that there are limited prospects of advancement. She wants a change of job basically because she needs more money. She is saving to get married. She isn't wearing an engagement ring because she and her financé wanted to save the money. Marlene favours not wearing a ring ('saves taking it off'). A single woman is a safer prospect to an employer, being less likely to leave to have children, and a ring could signal this possibility. Jeanine mentions advertising as a desirable line of work and is not very impressed when Marlene offers one job in a 'knitwear' marketing department and another at a promising concern selling 'lampshades'. Both are advances on her present position but they are evidently too mundane for Jeanine. She has a hazy notion of a job involving travelling, but no sense of a career structure ('I can't think about ten years'). Marlene strongly encourages her to go for one of the recommended jobs.

The scene shows Marlene at work. She wastes no time. She very quickly establishes what she needs to know about Jeanine in a professional context and smoothly moves her on. Jeanine has no focused ambition and Marlene, sensing her limitations, forcefully convinces her that the jobs she recommends are very worthwhile.

Act Two, Scene Two: Joyce's backyard – Sunday afternoon

The scene is Joyce's backyard. Squashed together in a shelter made of junk are Angie, who is sixteen, and Kit, who is twelve. The girls are hiding from Joyce (who appears to be Angie's mother) and ignore her calls from the house. Angie's disturbed animosity towards Joyce ('Wish she was dead') is reflected in her bullying of the younger Kit. She frightens Kit with stories of making pictures fall from the wall and hearing a dead kitten they know about; she accuses her of being timid, of being sexually ignorant, and her mother of being a slag. This clearly spills over from her unsatisfactory life with Joyce ('I'm going to kill my mother and you're going to watch' . . . 'If I don't get away from here I'm going to die'). They continue to ignore Joyce when she offers them a cup of tea and a biscuit. Kit, obviously fond of Angie, confides her fears of a possible war. Angie wants to go to London to see her aunt who is 'special' and 'gets people jobs' – thus establishing a possible connection with Marlene. She says that Joyce hates her aunt and, intriguingly, 'I think I'm my aunt's child. I think my mother's really my aunt'. The girls cuddle each other for comfort. Joyce comes down to the shelter where she knows the girls are hiding. Kit wants to go to the cinema but Joyce insists that Angie tidies her room first. Angie leaves reluctantly to do so, and Joyce talks about her concern for Angie to Kit. She sees little chance of her getting work when jobs are hard to get. 'She's one of those girls who might never leave home.' It worries Joyce that Angie plays with children much younger than herself, but she resents the suggestion that she is 'simple'. She is 'clever in her own way' and 'always kind to little children'. Kit is a confident young girl, conscious that she is clever. She mentions the possibility of becoming a nuclear physicist. Angie returns wearing an old best dress, slightly small for her. This inexplicable change of clothes irritates Joyce even more and she is yet more insistent that Angie cleans her room before anything else. Angie picks up a brick. When it begins to rain Joyce's harassment is compounded. She and Kit run into the house; Angie stays out in the rain. When Kit returns to fetch her in Angie says 'I put on this dress to kill my mother'.

Act Two, Scene Three: Employment Agency – Monday morning

The scene moves from a main office area to a small interviewing area and back again – the changes defined in the theatre by lighting.

Win and Nell have arrived at the 'Top Girls' Employment Agency on Monday morning. They drink coffee and discuss the weekend. Win has spent the weekend with a man at his home in West Sussex while his wife was away. Nell has been with two different men but won't be drawn to discuss her private life in detail. One of the men, Derek, has asked her again to marry him but she doesn't want to be tied down, 'to play house'. She prefers to work. They consider the position in the office now that Marlene has been promoted to Managing Director. Howard Kidd is upset because a woman has got the job he considered was his by right, because he is a man. The likelihood is that he will change his job. Nell would also like a change. She has had plenty of offers but 'most of them can't afford me. Or you' she says to Win. The two discuss their day's clients and are contemptuous of most of the men whose careers they are concerned with. One prospective client impresses them because her experience suggests she is a 'tough bird like us'.

Marlene arrives and Win and Nell applaud her promotion. Howard Kidd's resentment is again mentioned. Nell is dismissive of Win's secretive affair mentioned earlier ('Don't know why you bother'), and she is displeased that Marlene has been promoted rather than her ('I don't like coming second').

Interview: Louise and Win
Win's questions elicit the essential facts about Louise who, in two long speeches, succinctly defines the changing attitude of women to work.

She is embarrassed about her age. She is 46 but claims at first to be in her 'early forties'. Win acknowledges this is a handicap for women in business but is hopeful that Louise's experience will count in her favour. She explains that she has worked for the same company for twenty-one years and now wants to make a change. She deeply resents how she is taken for granted. Her mother has died, she has no social life, and she has come to the awful realisation that she is 'stuck there', having given her life to the company. She has been in middle management for twenty years and has built up an extremely efficient department. She has trained younger men who have gone on to higher things. Her work is always perfect and consequently nobody notices her. Now she wants to make them sorry to lose her. She would refuse any offer of more money that the Company might make. She has doubts about working with other women and believes that she passes as a man at work. She did take on one younger woman who had excellent qualifications and who progressed to being on the board of a competitor. Louise doesn't wholly approve of the new style she displayed. The new kind of attractive, well-dressed woman is not as careful as she had always been. They take themselves for granted whereas Louise has 'had to justify [her] existence every minute.' Win explains that any vacancies would be ones where Louise would be in competition with younger men. She offers one in a cosmetic company – a field easier for a woman – at a salary of £8,500 (less than Louise is currently earning). Louise is not so much concerned about money as about making a change. For her 'it's more important to get away'.

The Office

Marlene is working at her desk when Angie enters. Taken by surprise, Marlene does not recognise her at first. We soon make the connection that Angie is Marlene's niece and Joyce is her sister. Angie has come to London to visit her aunt and, hopefully, to stay with her. Marlene is not enthusiastic about this inconvenience, 'Unfortunately you've picked a day when I'm rather busy, if there's ever a day when I'm not'. Angie is overawed by the office and Marlene's status in it. Marlene explains that she is going to be in charge, and have a new office where 'there's just the one big desk in it for me'. Angie is thrilled ('I knew you'd be in charge of everything'). Marlene is anxious to know how long Angie intends to stay but Angie avoids giving a direct answer. She reminds Marlene of when she came to visit her and Joyce the year before. 'That was the best day of my whole life,' she says.

Howard Kidd's wife enters the office unannounced and is not at first recognised by Marlene. She assumes that Mrs Kidd wants to see her husband, Howard, but in fact she wants to talk to Marlene on a matter of some urgency. She notices Angie, who is introduced and who then retires to an inconspicuous part of the office where she overhears the conversation that ensues but takes no part in it. Mrs Kidd explains that Howard is in a state of shock about not getting the job of managing director. He is very upset and hasn't been able to sleep. The idea of working for a woman has appalled him and he has begun to denounce women in general, including his wife. She has had to take the blame. She has 'put him first every inch of the way' and now she warns Marlene that she will have to be very careful in her handling of him. Marlene listens to all this without much sympathy and, feeling that she is being reproached, she tries to cut the meeting short. She says she will treat Howard fairly and properly, and blames him for 'taking it out' on his wife. Mrs Kidd expresses her own, deeply felt opinion that what has happened is wrong. Howard Kidd has a family – a wife and three children – to support and it is only fair that he should have the job. Marlene begins to appreciate the real reason for Mrs Kidd's visit: that she might be persuaded to give up the job to Howard. She responds briskly and aggressively. She says that Howard has the choice of leaving if he isn't satisfied, and invites Mrs Kidd to leave. Mrs Kidd loses her self-control and, agreeing with her husband, she accuses Marlene of being 'one of these ballbreakers . . . You'll end up miserable and lonely. You're not natural'. Marlene tells her to 'please piss off', a crude, uncompromising dismissal which leaves Mrs Kidd with no alternative but to go.

Angie has heard this exchange and is immensely impressed by Marlene ('I think you were wonderful'). Marlene has to do some work and leaves Angie in the office which is 'where I most want to be in the world'.

Interview: Shona and Nell
Shona appears confident and successful. Nell's questions elicit that she is 29 (though young-looking), earning a healthy £9,000 annually selling for a company, but would like a change. Nell questions Shona on her attitude to selling and is assured that she has no qualms, no womanly hesitancy about concern for 'the customer's needs and his feelings'. Shona is uncompromising: she says 'I never consider people's feelings' and 'I'm not very nice'. She is interested in selling computers ('a top

field') or video systems ('a high-flying situation') and to the suggested salary of £10,000 to £15,000 and upwards she replies blandly 'Sounds OK'. The brash confidence of Shona's replies so impresses Nell, who recognises an equally ambitious career-woman, that she suggests the possibility of working for the 'Top Girls' agency sometime in the future ('We could keep in touch'). Shona is asked to describe her present job and she proceeds to recount a typical day – selling electrical goods in the North of England. Her exotic account of expense account living – driving a Porsche and staying in sophisticated hotels – gradually exposes her as a fraud. The picture is an unconvincing concoction of advertising cliches and fantasies. Nell says 'Not a word of this is true, is it?'. Shona turns out to be 21 and inexperienced – but unabashed when exposed by Nell.

The Office

Returning to the office, Win discovers Angie. Angie would like to work in the office but she has no formal qualifications at all. Asked what she can do she replies 'I don't know. Nothing.' In response to Angie's questions we hear Win's story. She had been headhunted by the 'Top Girls' agency who offered her more money than the firm she was working for, so she broke her contract. Her career began with a science degree and working in medical research, but she left to earn more money. She went abroad. She was always successful but, being a woman, her success made her unpopular. She would drink to cheer herself up. She soon discovered that she could do better than any of the men she worked with, who always made their work sound harder than it was. She lived with a man for four years and supported him as he couldn't get work. She went to California and enjoyed the sunshine and the life-style. Then to Mexico, still in 'sales', but it wasn't a suitable country for a single woman, so she came home. She went 'bonkers' for a time, thinking she was five different people, but recovered. The psychiatrist told her she was sane and very intelligent. She got married 'in a moment of weakness' but her husband has been in prison for the last four years and she doesn't visit him much any more. Win explains that she prefers working in the employment agency to selling because you can help people. Selling requires aggression and the customers don't usually want to meet you: 'It's no good if you like being liked'.

Nell and then Marlene re-enter the office. Nell reports that Howard Kidd has had a heart attack, but she is unaffected by the news: 'Lucky

he didn't get the job if that's what his health's like' she says. Win points
to Angie and remarks on her wish to work in the office. Marlene
dismisses any chance of future success for Angie: 'She's a bit thick.
She's a bit funny . . . she's not going to make it'.

Act Three: Joyce's kitchen – Sunday evening, a year earlier

Marlene has come to visit Joyce and Angie. She has brought some
presents. Angie, who is very excited, has opened a box of chocolates
and unwraps the dress which she had put on in Act Two, Scene Two.
Joyce has a present of perfume. Angie goes to her room to try on the
new dress. Joyce is unprepared for Marlene's visit and both sisters are
irritated by the discovery that Angie had invited Marlene without
letting Joyce know. There is a definite prickliness between the two.
When Angie reappears, thrilled about the new dress she is wearing, she
justifies her invitation on the grounds that she hasn't seen her aunt for
six years.

Kit enters to play with Angie but Angie, enchanted by the presence of
Marlene, won't go out and Kit leaves alone. Joyce explains that Kit is
like a little sister to Angie. She is the only girl who lives close to them
and Angie is 'good with little children'. Marlene wonders if Angie
might work with little children but Joyce dismisses the suggestion ('She
hasn't an idea in her head what she wants to do'). Marlene produces a
bottle of whisky and, offering Joyce a drink, remembers the last time
they drank together – the night their father died. Joyce still tends his
grave and visits their mother every week. They discuss local news and
Marlene learns that Joyce's husband 'moved out' three years previously.
These details add to the sense of Marlene's estrangement from her
family. Joyce remembers that Marlene was in America at the time.
Angie produces a post card which Marlene had sent them. The message
gives an image of Marlene's life that is far removed from the present
situation of drab domesticity: 'Driving across the States for a new job
in L.A. It's a long way but the car goes very fast. It's very hot'.

Angie's excitement at Marlene's visit irritates Joyce who sends Angie
to bed. Marlene is conscious of a deep resentment in Joyce and this
erupts when Marlene says that she has visited their aged mother that
day. Joyce visits their mother every week. Her bitterness focuses on
Marlene's leaving home 'Look, you've left, you've gone away,/we can
do without you'. The fraught situation develops into a furious

argument during which the facts of the past come tumbling out. Marlene left home to escape the awfulness of her parents' working-class existence. She got pregnant when 17 and let Joyce adopt the child. It seemed at the time that Joyce couldn't have children of her own. Angie is now confirmed as Marlene's daughter. Joyce later had a miscarriage because she was so exhausted looking after Marlene's baby. She hasn't been able to have any other children. Marlene has subsequently had two abortions. Eventually Marlene breaks down in tears and is comforted by Joyce ('Everyone's always crying in his house. Nobody takes any notice').

They talk about their men. Joyce's husband, Frank, was thrown out when he started having an affair with a younger woman ('He was always carrying on'). Joyce now has four different cleaning jobs in order to survive. She won't, however, accept financial help from Marlene. Marlene has always attracted men friends who like to be seen with a 'high-flying lady' but she won't conform to the required role of 'the little woman' at home. She prefers adventures and looks forward to the eighties which she thinks will be stupendous.

The sisters quarrel passionately about the immediate political situation in Britain, holding opposite views about the recent victory of Margaret Thatcher, the new Conservative Prime Minister. For Marlene this signals a new era of opportunity, when monetarist economic policy heralds revival and the individual with drive and initiative can prosper as never before. For Joyce, nothing has significantly changed. She reminds Marlene of the rotten life of their parents who were 'treated like rubbish': the mother went hungry and the father worked in the fields like an animal. She defends his domestic violence and his drinking as the inevitable consequence of his oppression. For Joyce 'nothing's changed and it won't with them in'. Marlene despises the working-class and Joyce loathes the wealthy people she has to work for. Marlene believes simply that 'Anyone can do anything if they've got what it takes', and Joyce points to Angie who is 'stupid, lazy and frightened' and asks what might be done for people like her. Joyce believes Angie's life is doomed to waste but Marlene thinks 'she'll be all right'. Joyce won't be reconciled and goes to bed, leaving Marlene alone. She sits wrapped in a blanket and has another drink. Angie comes in, calling for her mother. Marlene says, 'No, she's gone to bed. It's Aunty Marlene'. Angie speaks only one word, 'Frightening'.

Commentary

What Kind of Play?

A piece in the great Royal Court tradition: an angry, witty, front-line report on Britain, introducing characters and environments new to the theatre that affect all our lives. (Irving Wardle on Churchill's *Serious Money*, 1988)

If someone says 'a socialist playwright' or 'a feminist playwright' that can suggest to some people something rather narrow which doesn't cover as many things as you might be thinking about. (Caryl Churchill)

Max Stafford-Clark has directed an inchoate play, seemingly written on the principle 'I don't know what I think until I get it on paper.' (Francis King, 1982)

I don't set out to be a social writer, I just set out to write good plays, but I say that with the confidence that comes from knowing that they will have a social function. (Edward Bond)

Like Pope Joan, Caryl Churchill is something of a heresy. She is a major contemporary British dramatist and a woman. No woman playwright is included in Benedict Nightingale's *An Introduction to 50 Modern British Plays* (1982) which covers the twentieth century up to 1975. Only one appears among the fourteen dramatists in Methuen's two volumes of *Landmarks of Contemporary British Drama* (1986). Caryl Churchill is the one, and *Top Girls* is the play. Churchill features prominently in the numerous books on modern 'Feminist' or 'Political' theatre, but in interviews she is careful to avoid being pinned down to any limiting definition. The variety of her subject matter, the constant experiment with form and her challenge to conventional role models should serve as a warning to those who are keen to appropriate her for a cause or restrict in any way the scope of her drama.

The fact that it is a woman playwright who is experimenting in dramatic form enlivens critical analysis. Could it be that by challenging established models she is involved in creating a 'female' aesthetic? She is conscious of the possibility, but not driven by it:

> I remember before I wrote *Top Girls* thinking about women barristers – and how they were in a minority and had to imitate men to succeed – and I was thinking of them as different from me. And then I thought, 'wait a minute, my whole concept of what plays might be is from plays written by men . . .' And I remember long before that thinking of the 'maleness' of the traditional structure of plays, with conflict and building in a certain way to a climax. But it's not something I think about very often.

As Simon Trussler has concluded, the 'feminine' quality of her writing may simply have to do with dialectic replacing conflict, and open-endedness being preferred to climax.

The dialectic of *Top Girls* is wide ranging, covering universal dilemmas affecting women, but focuses on a major theme concerning contemporary life in Britain. Caryl Churchill has described the genesis of the play:

> The ideas for *Top Girls* came from all kinds of things. A lot of it went back a really long way. The idea of Dull Gret as a character I found in some old notebook from 1977 or 78. There'd been the idea of a play about a lot of dead women having coffee with someone from the present. And an idea about women doing all kinds of jobs. It was also that Thatcher had just become P.M.; and also I had been to America . . . and had been talking to women there who were saying things were going very well: they were getting far more women executives, women vice-presidents and so on. And that was such a different attitude from anything I'd met here, where feminism tends to be much more connected with socialism and not so much to do with women succeeding on the sort of capitalist ladder. All those ideas fed into *Top Girls*. I wanted it to set off, with all those historical women celebrating Marlene's achievement, to look as if it were going to be a celebration of women achieving things, and then to put the other perspectives on it, to show that just to achieve the same things that men had achieved in capitalist society wouldn't be a good object.

The critique of feminist ambitions is a clear central theme, but it is 'the other perspectives' which provide the richness of the play's treatment of the predicament of modern women. Churchill's selection of women characters from the past and the modern world shows sympathy for the feminist cause, disdaining the male oppressor, but there is no sentimentality or romanticism applied to any of them, and no comfortable solution offered for their problems. *Top Girls* confronts the audience with many questions, placing it firmly in that area of modern British theatre which believes the function of drama is to engage with immediate social issues.

There has been a shift in the theatre from plays where 'character' is fully explained; where psychological development of character is the main centre of interest and we are expected to know exactly why people do things. Modern British dramatists tend to give character and action a heightened social significance. This is particularly true of those playwrights who have been closely associated with the radical Royal Court theatre in London, or the variously 'committed' fringe and touring companies that emerged in the late 1960s and 70s. Caryl Churchill is pre-eminent among these writers. Chris Bigsby claims 'It is true to say that the single most significant development in British theatre in the decade 1968–1978 was the rise of socialist theatre.' This socialist theatre, a non-didactic political theatre, has involved the audience directly in judging not only the action but also, to an extent, themselves as part of the society which is being examined dramatically.

Many modern plays have consciously challenged the audience to question how they are reacting to what is being shown on stage. Edward Bond names his theatre 'a rational theatre' not because of any spoken dialectic or political argument but because his scenes and violent images demand of a rational audience the ability to find meaning and to make relevant connections. David Hare has explained that in *Plenty* (1978) the audience has to be actively engaged:

> I planned a play in twelve scenes, in which there would be twelve dramatic actions. Each of these actions is intended to be ambiguous, and it is up to the audience to decide what they feel about each event . . . This ambiguity is central to the idea of the play. The audience is asked to make its own mind up about each of the actions. In the act of judging the audience learns something about its own values. (A Note on Performance, *Plenty*, 1978)

Sympathy is not directed towards one character; sympathy shifts all the time. In Trevor Griffiths' *Comedians* (1975) a group of apprentice comedians try out their acts in a Northern club throughout Act Two. These acts are then adjudicated by a London agent in Act Three. However, the audience of the comedians in Act Two has, in reality, been the theatre audience, and, although the 'agent' is a dubious individual, it is the play's audience who are as much on trial as the would-be comedians. Their own reaction to the jokes of Act Two becomes inevitably integrated with the play's whole dialectic on the subject of comedy.

Similarly the varied images of women presented in *Top Girls* are bound to provoke strong reactions among a contemporary audience who cannot fail to recognise 'the very age and body of the time' and their place in it. In performance the play is disturbing, provocative and exuberant. Reacting to its first production the critic, John Elsom, wrote:

> It is splendid to see the Royal Court back in its old form, presenting virile plays on topical subjects, seizing our times by the scruff of the neck and shaking out the cant.

The Play World – A World of Women

> I am not a member of the Women's Rights League. Whatever I have written has been without any conscious thought of making propaganda. I have been more of a poet and less a social philosopher than people generally seem inclined to believe. I . . . must disclaim the honour of having consciously worked for the women's rights movement. I am not even quite clear as to just what this women's rights movement really is. To me it has seemed a problem of humanity in general. (Henrik Ibsen, 1898)

> We can now understand why there should be so many common features in the indictments drawn up against women, from the Greeks to our times. Her condition has remained the same through superficial changes, and it is this condition that determines what is called the 'character' of woman. (Simone de Beauvoir, *The Second Sex*)

The play world of *Top Girls* is a world of women's experience shown from a modern point of view. The settings are a restaurant, the 'Top Girls' Employment Agency and Joyce's backyard and kitchen. These are all specific locations set in England in the 1980s requiring careful physical representation on stage. But the 'play world' extends imaginatively to embrace the world of modern woman in all its variety, complexity and contrariness. Women dominate the locations of the play. They take over the restaurant of Act One; they have taken over the office (the traditional domain of the male) in Act Two; and they live in the kitchen (the traditional domain of the female) in Act Three. The locations become spaces where women can express themselves. The immediately striking feature of the play is that all the characters in it are women and no men appear on stage at all. Women are shown exclusively in relation to other women. Women are seen at work, discussing work. Unlikely women from the modern world are given a voice, as are women of different ages and different backgrounds, and a wider perspective is given by the younger generation of Angie and Kit. They all speak the language of women of today.

The Act One dinner guests from the past – 'a dramatic genealogy of Marlene's historical community' (Michelene Wandor) – are also, necessarily, a part of a *modern* scene. The actors will be recognised as modern women, their voices and movements modern; they speak modern English and they are the product of a modern imagination. When Lindsay Duncan acted Lady Nijo in the 1982 Royal Court production, she appeared as an English actress 'representing' a Japanese lady: no attempt was made to change the colour of her blonde hair. The women speak of experiences from the past, but they relate to Marlene and to each other as a sisterhood in the present. All the other women in the play are contemporary figures supposedly alive in the England of the early 1980s.

The depiction of these women is in sharp contrast with the traditional, or 'classical', representation of women in plays. In the past women characters have been presented almost exclusively as adjuncts to men, dependent on men and limited by the rules and conventions of a male dominated world. Their dramatic 'roles' have been severely restricted – as wives, daughters, lovers, harlots – always contingent on men, rarely permitted to act or think independently. Even in the nineteenth century, when Ibsen and Strindberg wrote about strong-minded women, their characters were always inseparable from men. The modern woman is shown in *Top Girls* to be living at a time of shifting priorities and expectations as far as women are concerned. Female 'roles' can be challenged. The play is original in presenting so many different kinds of women, and letting them speak for themselves. The characters are 'types' to a certain extent, representational, but they are always individualised, dramatically interesting, and they open up a world of experience new to the British stage.

Themes and Context

The New Woman

The many ideas, themes and motifs that run throughout *Top Girls* relate to the time when the play was written. All plays deal with shared assumptions and a shared experience drawn from the social context. The dramatist organises meaning in the structure of the play and the audience uses its own experience to find the play's significance. Not everything has to be explained in the narrative because the dramatist can assume that the audience will fill in the gaps. For this reason it is useful to know something of the shared context if a play is to be understood. A simple example is that of the name 'Maggie', referred to by Marlene in Act Three. Caryl Churchill can assume with confidence that her audience will know that Maggie refers to Margaret Thatcher, and she need not use the full name in the play. Similarly, a much wider range of assumptions about life in Britain in the 1970s underlies *Top Girls* and should be considered.

Britain in the 1970s witnessed a profound change in the consciousness of women as a group. Perhaps for the first time changes in law, in publishing and the media, in the arts, in attitudes to public morality and in social habits combined in a relatively short period to alter radically the base from which women viewed their lives. *Top Girls*, which carries a sense and a mood of driving fast into the 1980s, assumes this change of consciousness. Marlene, Win and Nell – the young women executives of the 'Top Girls' Agency – do not discuss radical feminism; for them, apparently, there is no need. They are not intimidated by men. Far from it. They expect to do everything that men do, and to do it better. Louise, however, recognises that a change has taken place and that there is a woman now who is different from her generation. 'She has a different style, she's a new kind . . . a kind of woman who is thirty now who grew up in a different climate.' How did this climate come about? What produced the new woman?

Publishing was important. Seminal polemical writings such as

Germaine Greer's *The Female Eunuch*, Kate Millett's *Sexual Politics* and Eva Figes' *Patriarchal Attitudes*, all published in 1970, were best-sellers and widely influenced the feminist consciousness. Mary Stott began to edit a serious Woman's Page in the *Guardian* newspaper. Two new publishing houses began to raise the profile of women's writing. In 1973 The Virago Press began to reclaim and promote significant woman writers of the past as well as the present. In 1975 The Women's Press began with a more radical and more international list of feminist writers. Both companies used easily identifiable book covers which became a prominent feature on the shelves of bookshops throughout Britain. For the first time women were able to make editorial decisions at the highest level. Four feminist journals were established in 1972.

Legislation specifically affecting women is not a recent phenomenon but it mushroomed in the 1970s. Several Acts of Parliament had a sudden and major influence on women's changing sense of personal independence and their relationship with employment. In 1967 The Abortion Act made abortion far easier to obtain; in 1969 The Divorce Reform Act broadened grounds for divorce; in 1970 The Equal Pay Act stipulated that equal pay for men and women doing the same job was to become law; in 1974 contraceptives were made freely available on the National Health Service; and in 1975 The Sex Discrimination Act banned sex discrimination in employment, education and advertising and set up the Equal Opportunities Commission to see that the new Act was observed. Also the Employment Protection Act guaranteed pregnant women their jobs after maternity leave.

The Women's Liberation Movement was formally active in Britain throughout the 1970s and did much to focus attention on women's issues and to raise women's consciousness of themselves as a group with identifiable demands and needs. Feminism was not so concerned with gaining equality with men – the law was moving in that direction – but with the right to self-determination. Feminism questions any assumption that women are secondary and dependent on men and that the social and sexual division of labour is natural and unchanging. During the 1970s feminists were very successful in the encouragement of pressure groups formed to support the interests of women in their own areas of employment – in the Civil Service, in Industry, in Medicine. For the general public perhaps the most evident change was the raising of the profile of women in broadcasting – as newsreaders, presenters, and interviewers on serious programmes.

Arguing that 'the personal is political' feminism challenges both male dominance and female passivity. 'Patriarchy' has, nevertheless, proved a formidable obstacle to women. This is not surprising, given its deeply entrenched history. Patriarchy involves more than a chauvinistic 'attitude'. Hartman defines patriarchy as 'a set of social relations between men, which have a material base, and which, though hierarchical, establish or create interdependence and solidarity among men that enable them to dominate women'. Patriarchy might explain why 98 per cent of the top salary earners in Britain are men. It has a profound relevance to *Top Girls*, both regarding the play's sexual politics and its treatment of the subject of employment.

The first audiences for *Top Girls* would have absorbed the changes in law and in thinking that occurred during the 1970s in relation to women and would react to the play in the light of this knowledge. The play, begun in 1979, and performed in 1982, is an incisive and reflective response to the immediate times; and, being closely related to the present, it is fully conscious of the immediate future.

Act One

The long spectacular dinner scene of Act One introduces feminist themes which are to echo throughout the play and, as the play is constantly offering shifting perspectives, so the first scene is full of contradictions. The occasion is the formal celebration of Marlene's promotion to the position of Managing Director of the 'Top Girls' Employment Agency ('Over all the women you work with. And all the men.') and the celebration expands to include all the guests:

> MARLENE. We've all come a long way. To our courage and the way we changed our lives and our extraordinary achievements. (*They laugh and drink a toast.*) (p. 13)

There is much good humour, mutual congratulation and enjoyment among the group as might be expected. However the celebratory mood is regularly undercut by details of individual suffering, and the scene moves gradually towards chaos. By the end the guests, mostly drunk, are lost in personal reminiscence, and while Isabella remembers her last triumph ('How marvellous while it lasted') Joan is actually being sick. The disintegration of the party is extremely ironic. Dull Gret's final, apocalyptic vision of collective female action ('We're going to where the evil comes from and pay the bastards out') is set against the stage picture of a group of women no longer listening to each other. The visual statement anticipates the play's final recognition that the condition of women has changed only superficially and that individual triumphs are relative and marginal. Not least of the scene's ironies is the regular appearance of the nameless waitress who serves the dinner: a modern working woman completely ignored as an individual by the party of women achievers.

There is no difficulty in accepting the presence of the five women from the past in a modern restaurant. Theatre invites us to suspend disbelief, and few of us, even now, have trouble accepting ghosts or witches in Shakespeare. The arrival of the guests on stage is both surprising and vastly entertaining. There is an element of cabaret and fancy dress which is good fun. The five guests are, nevertheless, a carefully selected group. Nijo and Isabella Bird are known because of their autobiographical writing and Joan, Griselda and Gret each achieved mythical status in their own right. The women are clearly distinguished on stage by their costume, but it soon emerges that they are also temperamentally very different. Their dramatic function is partly to represent different aspects of the female psyche and partly to suggest a universal female experience. Collectively they provide an historical context for the new woman who is represented in this scene by Marlene. History, which has traditionally dealt predominantly with men and been written by men, is here given a feminist perspective.

As the play progresses and Marlene's history is revealed, she emerges as a particular kind of new woman – career-minded, determined and ambitious. Other modern characters differ in their values. The five remarkable women from the past also reveal contrasting female values. Isabella is adventurous, keen on the outdoors and actually made ill by domesticity; Nijo is concerned with social convention and her place at court (symbolised by her preoccupation with clothes); Joan is intellectual – fascinated by ideas and philosophical debate; Gret is the least sophisticated – a grotesque creature of appetite, almost a parody of the peasant woman and Griselda epitomises the submissive and dutiful wife and mother, happy in her obedience. There is much witty entertainment in performance from the interplay of these contrasting personalities. From Nijo's snobbery, for example,

ISABELLA. There are some barbaric practices in the east.
NIJO. Barbaric?
ISABELLA. Among the lower classes.
NIJO. I wouldn't know. (p. 6)

And from Isabella's discretion ('I knew coming to dinner with a Pope
we should keep off religion' and 'I did think it was remarkably barbaric
to kill them but you learn not to say anything'). Altogether the marked
differences of personality mitigate against any simple 'definition' of
what constitutes a woman.

However, the stories of Act One, drawn from different times and
different social backgrounds, point to a universal female experience of
oppression. It would appear that women have always been expected to
fulfil certain roles, regardless of individual temperament, and have been
excluded from other experiences and possibilities in life. The roles have
been determined for the convenience of men. Nijo and Griselda were
essentially slaves in their time, albeit willing in their service. Joan was
forced to adopt a disguise in order to satisfy her aspiration for
knowledge. She says 'I shouldn't have been a woman. Women, children
and lunatics can't be Pope.' The irony is that she was perfectly
acceptable as Pope before the truth was found out. Then she was killed
for being a woman. Isabella was expected to lead the life of a
clergyman's daughter and always felt guilty when she attempted to
break free. Her frustration is all too clear:

ISABELLA. How can people live in this dim pale island and wear our
  hideous clothes? I cannot and will not live the life of a lady . . .
  Why should I? Why should I? (p. 26)

Throughout the dinner Marlene provides a modern, liberated
commentary on the stories from the past, and she is particularly
scathing about Griselda's experience of the dreadful Walter ('I can't
stand this' she says). By the end the guests form a chorus of
disapproval. Nijo repeats her one gesture of defiance – 'I hit him with a
stick' – and even Griselda begins to have second thoughts – 'I do think
– I do wonder – it would have been nicer if Walter hadn't had to.' The
feeling of resentment is given most powerful expression in Gret's
description of her own feminist revolution. All the details of
persecution – rape, loss of children, eviction – build to a climax in her
story:

GRET. . . . I'd had enough, I was mad, I hate the bastards. I come
out of my front door that morning and shout till my neighbours
come out and I said, 'Come on, we're going . . . (p. 28)

By now none of the guests is in any state to join in organised opposition
to anything, and Joan least of all. Her drunken state and the group
picking up on certain Latin phrases ('O miseras!') is invariably the
source of laughter in the theatre. But how significant is Joan's Latin,
given that it is rarely understood in the theatre? Taken from Lucretius,
it advocates withdrawal from worldly involvement – 'nothing is more
delightful than to occupy the calm of an ivory tower built on the
teachings of wise men'. (See the full translation on p. 91.) Greg
Giesekam has suggested the intriguing possibility that:

> Far from being irrelevant, these Latin verses provide an ironic
> counterpoise to the socialist-feminist dynamic of the play, with their
> stance of individual satisfaction based on inaction contrasted with
> Gret's participation in collective action. The irony of the contrast is
> heavily underscored by Joan's drunken state as she delivers the lines
> – her 'templa' of wisdom have hardly proved 'serena'. (Studies in
> Theatre Production, January 1990)

However, this is surely making excessive demands on a modern
audience and it is unlikely that Caryl Churchill intended quite that level
of dramatic irony. The implicit question behind all the stories of
iniquities that women have had to put up with in the past focuses on
the possibility of change. The presence of the modern 'successful'
Marlene suggests that the problems of the past are confined to the past,
but this is not entirely true. Marlene asks 'Don't you get angry? I get
angry.' The modern women of the play also have to cope with the
endemic enigma of being women in a society where so many standards
have been set by men. Act Three, through the character of Joyce,
suggests that the only fundamental change for the better – for both
women and men – must come through a change in political thinking.
Act One gives expression to a universal female resentment which
continues on various levels throughout the play.

Resentment about one's lot in life is most obviously expressed in
anger, and many women in Top Girls are angry, but alternatives to the
characters' present circumstances are unclear and the general
frustration, introduced in Act One, becomes a motif of wanting to 'get

away'. Nijo travelled for twenty years; Jeanine would like to travel and
Shona wants to be on the road; Isabella couldn't stay in Scotland and
always felt dull when stationary; Win has travelled widely; Louise feels
the most important thing for her is to 'get away'. Angie says 'If I don't
get away from here I'm going to die'. Nobody, however, expresses a
stronger need to get away than Marlene does – from what was her
family and their background – 'I knew when I was thirteen, out of their
house, out of them . . .' At one extreme this is a reaction to an
intolerable situation, but it can also express a need for something new,
for adventure. The instinct is complex and unresolved. Marlene's
opening words to Isabella introduce the dilemma. She has just achieved
a desired promotion and now 'I haven't time for a holiday. I'd like to
go somewhere exotic like you but I can't get away . . . I'd like to lie in
the sun forever, except of course I can't bear sitting still.'

Women and Work
Top Girls is the name of the employment agency where most of Act
Two takes place. Employees and clients reflect different attitudes
towards careers and the subject of women at work becomes a major
concern of the play. Work is an essential fact of life for the modern
women who appear in Act Two. Again, the social context provides a
useful background to these characters.

   In the 1970s and early 1980s social changes in Britain did affect
women in relation to employment but the national pattern was, in fact,
relatively unshifting. The play recognises this. If salary were taken as
the measuring point there were very few 'top girls'. The Policy Studies
Institute (1981), examining women in top jobs found that:

> If 'high earners' among employees are defined as the top 2½–3% of
> all who are employed full time, women accounted for just under
> 2% in 1979. At the highest earnings levels they are scarcely
> represented at all.

Furthermore, despite equal opportunities legislation, women remain
concentrated at the bottom of the hierarchies of pay and promotion
opportunities. This is partly because women often choose employment
in professions that do not offer high salaries (for example in education,
health and welfare, and mostly in clerical occupations) and partly
because so many women work part-time.

Against this stark reality, however, changes were taking place which are reflected in the play and are relevant to it. At a time of sharp decline in male employment, notably in manufacturing industries, women's employment was increasing nationally. This was especially so in 'service' industries – of which the 'Top Girls' Employment Agency is an excellent example. More women became available for work in the 1970s, and with girls and women gaining more academic and vocational qualifications all the time, they became more competitive in the labour market ('There's not a lot of room upward' says Nell). Forty five per cent of all waged workers in Britain are women, and the play offers a challenging social perspective – from Marlene's admired new woman:

MARLENE. I know a managing director who's got two children, she breast feeds in the board room, she pays a hundred pounds a week on domestic help alone and she can afford that because she's an extremely high-powered lady earning a great deal of money.
(p. 80)

to the other extreme of Joyce, who has four cleaning jobs – which she hates – and Angie who might become a 'packer in Tesco' but certainly is 'not going to make it'.

Economic independence is a *sine qua non* of women's liberation. As Virginia Woolf recognised in 1928 – 'A woman must have money and a room of her own if she is to write fiction.' During the 1970s changes in social life-style affected the labour market. Women had fewer children. For the first time the birth rate fell below the death rate in Britain. Women had their first child later and their last child sooner, and so the time spent bearing and raising children declined. A shift in the moral climate made single mothers acceptable, and reduced the pressure on young people to marry and have children. Together with an increase in the divorce rate these changes placed more women in need of economic independence and available for work.

The victim mentality of the isolated and housebound wife and mother was challenged during the 1970s. While it remains true that most housework is still carried out by women, the basic drudgery has been relieved by mechanical aids, freeing women for other things. The proliferation nationally of social activities organised for women helped take women out of the house. Health clubs, fitness classes, dancing, aerobics and such like activities brought women together and developed

women's consciousness of possible alternatives. The traditional
domestic role has no appeal whatsoever for Nell in *Top Girls*:

>NELL. Derek asked me to marry him again.
>WIN. He doesn't know when he's beaten.
>NELL. I told him I'm not going to play house, not even in Ascot.
>WIN. Mind you, you could play house.
>NELL. If I chose to play house I would play house ace.
>WIN. You could marry him and go on working.
>NELL. I could go on working and not marry him. (p. 48)

The key problem for professional women in Britain has always been the
difficulty of reconciling a career with a family. Access to top jobs is
easier for those women who have few or no family responsibilities.
This, of course, is a major issue in *Top Girls*.

Act Two

The scenes in the 'Top Girls' employment agency and the varied cross-
section of women who appear in them develop the subject of women
and work. In earlier editions of the play there are only two acts,
allowing for one interval during performance after the third scene. In
her revised structure Churchill makes the central three scenes a discrete
act (Act Two), and calls it 'Angie's story'. The character Angie has the
function of extending the significance of the office scenes to the world
outside, posing awkward questions about the nature of 'success' and
the aspirations of the women who work in the office.

Many modern plays invite the audience to judge an action which
might not be fully explained on stage. The structure of the plays
provides coherence and meaning, but the perceptiveness of the audience
is required to draw relevant conclusions. Where more is involved than
the literal words and actions the dominating method is irony. Irony
often begins with the title of the play, as in Edward Bond's *Saved*,
which disputes the notion of 'Christian' salvation, or David Hare's
Plenty, where the post-war optimism of the ending is placed in ironic
juxtaposition with the play's earlier picture of a declining England.
Similarly the title *Top Girls* is ironic. The play is less concerned with
the celebration of successful women than with questioning the kind of
success that is shown. Benedict Nightingale recognised the central
questions of the play:

What use is female emancipation, Churchill asks, if it transforms the clever women into predators and does nothing for the stupid, weak and helpless? Does freedom, and feminism, consist of aggressively adopting the very values that have for centuries oppressed your sex? (*New Statesman*, 1982)

These questions are not debated in the form of dialogue but are posed by the action on stage. In particular, the office scenes are equivocal in performance. There is a definite glamour to be found in the physical surroundings, in the appearance of the smart young women executives, and in the reversal of normal proceedings – with the office being run entirely by women who are able to shape the careers of men as well as women. However, the attitude of these successful women – Marlene, Win and Nell – is open to question. A similar ambiguity occurs in Churchill's later *Serious Money* (1987) where the energy and buzz projected by the City financial dealers at work generates excitement, but what we see is pure greed and egotism.

The dialogue in the 'Top Girls' office reflects a dismissive attitude to clients and even colleagues. Win and Nell cherish those who might be 'tough birds', like them, but otherwise their tone is harsh and unfeeling. One client is 'Pushy. Bit of a cowboy . . . not overbright', another is rejected as 'that poor little nerd'; ambitious young men are 'really pretty bastards'; potential female employees are relegated to 'half a dozen little girls'; their colleague, Howard Kidd, ('Poor little bugger') suffers a heart attack and Nell's response is simply 'Lucky he didn't get the job if that's what his health's like'. Nell, in her interview with Shona, admits to her own aggressiveness:

NELL. And what about closing?

SHONA. I close, don't I?

NELL. Because that's what an employer is going to have doubts
    about with a lady as I needn't tell you, whether she's got the guts
    to push through to a closing situation. They think we're too nice.
    They think we listen to the buyer's doubts. They think we consider
    his needs and his feelings.

SHONA. I never consider people's feelings.

NELL. I was selling for six years, I can sell anything, I've sold in
    three continents, and I'm jolly as they come but I'm not very nice.
    (p. 61)

In her interview with Jeanine, Marlene displays her professionalism – her experience, her astuteness and her pragmatism. She is able to sum-up Jeanine from an employer's point of view in half a minute, finds her limited, and then moves her on forcefully and efficiently. She has no personal interest in Jeanine, and finding her naive she wastes no more time than is necessary on her; she encourages Jeanine to get one of the proffered jobs, but her claim 'I'm putting myself on the line for you' is not true.

The office women have achieved relative success and independence but within a system created essentially by men. The system is hierarchical (hence *Top Girls*), and within a capitalist economy it is the fittest who survive. Marlene, Win and Nell may be dismissive of men ('Men are awful bullshitters'), and they are certainly clever and able, but they have done nothing to challenge patriarchal authority. By achieving positions of power and responsibility they have appropriated it within the system. The determination and ruthlessness shown in the office indicates that they have had to adopt the kind of behaviour that women have traditionally resented in men.

Furthermore, the office scenes give a clear picture that women's professional horizons are limited, even today. Win reflects that 'there's not many top ladies about' and 'there's nothing going here' in the office. Jeanine and Louise add further perspective to the problem of women and employment when they are interviewed for jobs. Neither is offered much that is encouraging. Jeanine is offered two positions: marketing knitwear at an increased salary of £110 per week (a minimal improvement on her present post), or secretarial and reception duties in a small firm producing lampshades, with some prospects but no increase in salary at all. Louise is forty-six and more mature, experienced and commanding than Jeanine. She is advised to look towards 'fields that are easier for a woman', and she might have to accept a drop in salary in order to change her life. Win is realistic and frank with her. 'Let's face it, vacancies are going to be ones where you'll be in competition with younger men'.

The chances, therefore, of becoming a 'top' girl under the existing competitive economic system are shown to be difficult, and the achievement questionable. For the less forceful (Jeanine and Louise) the opportunities appear to be clearly limited. However, with the character of Angie in Act Two, the play exposes how divisive the system is by taking into account the situation of the helpless: of those who are quite incapable of entering the scramble for worthwhile employment – those from poor social backgrounds. Joyce knows that 'She's not going to get a job when jobs are hard to get'. Hopeless at school, without any formal qualifications, lazy and disturbed, Angie can also be described as a victim. While the successful look after themselves, who is there in society to look after Angie? Joyce struggles to survive and can barely cope with her. There is no sentimentality attached to the presentation of Angie, yet she is shown to be affectionate and possessed of a vivid emotional life. Her frustration and longing are eloquent testimony to the cost of others' 'success', and her presence in the office poignantly undermines the image of individualistic achievement.

Angie may be the ultimate victim of a competitive society, but the range of women who are shown in the office suggests that employment is a real cause of concern for women in general. The play doesn't say that women should not go to work – clearly they need to and want to – but work inevitably affects the whole of their lives, and frequently for the worse. Those who appear to have succeeded are all 'travelling light', having rejected family responsibilities. They are not entirely happy. Nell resents Marlene's success, Win is lonely, and Marlene – who thinks it is 'very good' to have her own office – has abandoned her daughter. The entry of Mrs Kidd highlights another dilemma of employment. In some respects she is an anachronism, quite out of place and uncomfortable in this office, and her request for Marlene to give up her new job is unreasonable ('He's got a family to support. He's got three children. It's only fair.'), but she does represent another point of view. Marlene treats her harshly, but Mrs Kidd's accusation that she is 'not natural' carries the weight of traditional opinion that the woman's place is in the home. This prejudice is one more difficulty that professional women have to face, even from other women.

Women and Politics

Our policies are perfectly right. There will be no change. (13.8.1980 Margaret Thatcher)

There are good times very much in prospect. (25.1.1987 Margaret Thatcher)

There is no such thing as society. There are individual men and women and there are families. (1.11.1987 Margaret Thatcher)

Women are soft, mild, pitiful and flexible;
Thou stern, obdurate, flinty, rough, remorseless.
(William Shakespeare, *Henry VI*, Ptiii, ll. 141–42)

Top Girls was written and performed during the early years of Margaret Thatcher's first term as Prime Minister of Great Britain. The policies and principles of her Conservative government are the immediate political context of the play and emerge in Act Three as the focus of the impassioned quarrel between Marlene and Joyce. Thatcher is Marlene's heroine and very much the 'top girl'.

Thatcher was elected leader of the Conservative Party – the first woman to be so – in 1975, having challenged Edward Heath for the job. She became Prime Minister in 1979 – the first woman in British history to hold this position – and won another two elections during the 1980s. From the beginning her government was associated with radical right-wing economic policies which were to have profound social consequences. Thatcher's government pursued monetarist policies to control inflation. To this end the money supply was to be reduced and public spending reined in. State socialism would be rolled back by the privatisation of major nationalised industries, and the power of the unions would be broken by new legislation. Individual initiative would be stimulated by lower direct taxation and the injection of competitive market forces in many areas of public life.

In *Top Girls* Marlene embraces the 'enterprise culture' encouraged by Thatcher and supports monetarism regardless of the social consequences. Joyce and Angie represent that section of society most in need of social support. Their future does not appear hopeful.

Perhaps the greatest irony operating in the play is the phenomenon of Margaret Thatcher. Few women in history have broken more taboos than she has, by becoming leader of the Conservative Party and Prime Minister of Great Britain. The socialist bias of the play, however, cannot allow this achievement to go unchallenged.

Act Three

Act Three fills out Marlene's story and in so doing moves the feminist themes of the play into the arena of contemporary politics. As Joyce says angrily to Marlene – 'you've got on, nothing's changed for most people, has it?' While Marlene is confirmed as an advocate for 'Thatcherism' Joyce argues that fundamental change can only be achieved by socialism. The argument is more implied than stated.

Joyce has had a bad experience of men and is quite disenchanted by them ('I'd sooner do without') but her argument shifts the history of sexual oppression into a wider social context:

JOYCE. You say Mother had a wasted life.

MARLENE. Yes I do. Married to that bastard.

JOYCE. What sort of life did he have? / Working in the fields like

MARLENE. Violent life?

JOYCE. an animal. / Why wouldn't he want a drink?

MARLENE. Come off it.

JOYCE. You want a drink. He couldn't afford whisky.

MARLENE. I don't want to talk about him.

JOYCE. You started, I was talking about her. She had a rotten life
because she had nothing. She went hungry.

MARLENE. She was hungry because he drank the money. / He used
to hit her.

JOYCE. It's not all down to him / Their lives were rubbish. They

MARLENE. She didn't hit him.

JOYCE. were treated like rubbish. He's dead and she'll die soon and
what sort of life / did they have? (p. 84–5)

Joyce, by referring to 'people' rather than 'women' in her argument,
focuses on her experience of vertical class distinctions – the traditional
demarcation between rich and poor. Class structure is seen by her as
the cause of oppression. The political row between the fraught sisters is
exaggerated and simplified ('MARLENE: I hate the working class . . .'
'JOYCE: I spit when I see a Rolls Royce . . .') but as it encompasses
much of the 'State of England' drama of the 1960s and 1970s it can
afford to be. A contemporary 1982 audience would have been well
versed in the political debate. Nevertheless, the weight of the play's
argument reaches a climax where political realities cannot be avoided,
and Joyce is finally alienated from Marlene by her political sympathies:

MARLENE. . . . I don't believe in class. Anyone can do anything if
they've got what it takes.

JOYCE. And if they haven't?

MARLENE. If they're stupid or lazy or frightened, I'm not going to
help them get a job, why should I?

JOYCE. What about Angie?

MARLENE. What about Angie?

JOYCE. She's stupid, lazy and frightened, so what about her?

MARLENE. You run her down too much. She'll be all right.

JOYCE. I don't expect so, no. I expect her children will say what a

> wasted life she had. If she has children. Because nothing's changed
> and it won't with them in.
> MARLENE. Them, them. / Us and them?
> JOYCE. And you're one of them. (p. 86)

Marlene has managed by her own determination and effort to lift
herself out of working-class deprivation, and while her achievement as
an individual can be admired (as it is in Act One) the facts pertaining to
Angie and Joyce place her success in another light.

Marlene expresses wholehearted support for Thatcher – 'She's a
tough lady, Maggie. I'd give her a job . . . Monetarism is not stupid . . .
Certainly gets my vote' – and her own success could be seen to
vindicate the encouragement of individual initiative. However, Act
Three reveals aspects of her life which we must question. She left home
without a backward glance. By handing Angie to Joyce she made the
symbolic gesture of cutting herself off from family and family
responsibility. She hasn't visited 'home' for six years. Angie's arrival in
the office (Act Two) is clearly an inconvenience to her, and Marlene
wishes she was out of the way. Nevertheless, sympathy is carefully
balanced in the play. Joyce is not presented as an heroic working-class
survivor, fighting for socialism. In many respects she is a failure, worn
down by the sheer drudgery of her existence, let down by her husband,
and struggling with mixed success to look after Angie. The history of
the sisters' social and family background is as grim as anything
recounted in Act One. Marlene determined to 'get out', Joyce decided
to stay. The play questions that these choices have to be made at all in
the modern world, given the cost to all concerned.

Language

Top Girls is a language-oriented play. Characters engage above all in
talk. Language patterns vary: the play offers excited or furious
overlapping dialogue; incisive questioning giving way to the set speech;
different codes and registers defining contrasting social groups. The
retroactive last scene and the fact that ten characters appear only once
indicates that psychological development through the play is not a
priority. More important is what the characters represent and what
they have to say. The distinctive quality of the language of *Top Girls* is

its clarity and incisiveness and how sensitive the text is to live performance.

In performance an actor uses more than words to present a character but the words come first. An actor employs body language; she wears costume appropriately defining her professional or social situation; and also, very importantly, she will speak with an accent, a tone of voice and quality and texture of sound that defines her social background as well as her mood. Caryl Churchill provides for this very precisely in the written text, which becomes the spoken language of the play.

Top Girls includes different social groups in contemporary Britain and recognises changes that are occurring within the traditional parameters. The social background of the modern characters is always significant and their speech shows what this is. Initially the names of the characters help to place them. Marlene's appearance and voice would signal instant impressions as the play opens, but a vital clue – absorbed almost unconsciously by an English audience – is given when Nijo calls her by name. Marlene is mostly a working-class name in Britain. Similarly Jeanine, Shona, Joyce and the diminutive 'Angie' (Joyce uses 'Marley' to comfort Marlene) fit comfortably in a 'lower' class background. Rosemary and Howard Kidd have first names associated more often with the middle class. Mrs Kidd is the only modern character in the play who has a surname. She is identified absolutely in relation to her husband, whose name she has taken. In her brief scene she speaks for a substantial social group – the stay-at-home wife, comfortably off, who services her husband and children. Win and Nell are more difficult to place; their names are socially ambiguous. They represent the new class, based on capitalist enterprise, which is accessible to the aspiring Marlene.

As in all plays that are set in modern Britain, the class or social group of a character is important. Conventionally in the theatre different social groups have been defined most obviously by their manner of speech. Since the late 1950s British playwrights have focused a great deal on the working-class, providing stage space and a voice for that lower social group which has traditionally in 'middle class' plays been relegated to stereotypes, often of a comic variety. A patronising element, evident in the opening of Noël Coward's 1941 *Blithe Spirit*, for example, has been banished from the modern stage. Here the sophisticated Ruth is giving instructions to the maid Edith:

RUTH. And when you're serving dinner, Edith, try to remember to
do it calmly and methodically.

EDITH. Yes'm.

RUTH. As you are not in the Navy it is unnecessary to do everything
at the double.

EDITH. Very good, 'm.

RUTH. Now go and get the ice.

EDITH. (*straining at the leash*): Yes'm.
She starts off at full speed.

RUTH. *Not* at a run, Edith.

EDITH. (*slowing down*): Yes'm.
Edith goes

The 'off-stage' existence of an Edith character is of no consequence at
all, while the audience is invited to take vicarious pleasure in the social
ease, wit, and superiority of the Ruth character. The British theatre of
the 60s and 70s went a long way towards reversing this social
sympathy, making the working-class a serious subject of concern.
Television drama has sustained a sense of unchanging class divisions
through classic serials, period plays and soap operas, but modern
theatre has challenged the fixedness of class by making the
representatives of the working-class articulate.

The working-class has consistently been represented by the use of
vernacular speech which, in English, can be remarkably varied. Arnold
Wesker, for example, uses a Norfolk dialect in *Roots* (1959):

MRS BRYANT. I shall never forget when I furse hear on it. I was in
the village and I was talking to Reggie Fowler. I say to him,
there've bin a lot o' talk about Jimmy ent there? Disgustin', I say.

Harold Pinter, in *The Caretaker* (1961), employs a more stylised
vernacular which, in performance, again requires the actors to consider
the appropriate accent:

ASTON. You Welsh?
Pause

DAVIES. Well, I been around, you know . . . what I mean . . . I been
about . . .

ASTON. Where were you born then?

DAVIES. (*darkly*) What do you mean?

ASTON. Where were you born?

DAVIES. I was . . . uh . . . oh, it's a bit hard, like, to set your mind
   back . . . see what I mean . . . going back . . . a good way . . . lose
   a bit of track, like . . . you know . . .

An extreme example of local speech, again stylised, is found in Nigel
Williams' classroom drama *Class Enemy* (1978), where phonetic
spelling is used to denote the sound:

SKY-LIGHT. Woss in store eh? I wonder. Woss in store?
IRON. Fuck all's in store.
RACKS. Why we stay Sky-Light?
SKY-LIGHT. Sunning ter do innit.

All these plays have a strong basis in a specific place and the characters
reflect that in their speech. The scenes in *Top Girls* are brought vividly
to life by an accurate and varied re-creation of codes of speech equally
rooted in time and place. The close relationship between Angie and Kit
is made convincing by a recognition of children's insecurities, their
range of reference, and – mostly usefully for the actors involved – by
the continuous reference to themselves in the immediate present
through the repetition of personal pronouns:

KIT. My mum don't like you anyway.
ANGIE. I don't want her to like me. She's a slag.
KIT. She is not.
ANGIE. She does it with everyone.
KIT. She does not.
ANGIE. You don't even know what it is.
KIT. Yes I do.
ANGIE. Tell me then.
KIT. We get it all at school, cleverclogs. It's on television. You
   haven't done it.
ANGIE. How do you know?
KIT. Because I know you haven't
ANGIE. You know wrong then because I have. (p. 36–7)

A similar domestic intimacy is conveyed between Marlene and Joyce,
again by the use of 'I', 'you' and 'we' to emphasise the personal nature
of the dialogue:

MARLENE. How do you mean you didn't know I was coming?
JOYCE. You could have written. I know we're not on the phone but
   we're not completely in the dark ages, / we do have a postman.

MARLENE. But you asked me to come.

JOYCE. How did I ask you to come?

MARLENE. Angie said when she phoned up. (p. 68–9)

In contrast the 'Top Girls' office executives engage in a sharp-edged knowing banter which manages to show how they are closely linked and yet, at the same time, keeping themselves at a personal distance from each other:

NELL. . . . I've got that poor little nerd I should never have said I could help. Tender heart me.

WIN. Tender like old boots. How old?

NELL. Yes well forty-five.

WIN. Say no more.

NELL. He knows his place, he's not after calling himself a manager, he's just a poor little bod wants a better commission and a bit of sunshine.

WIN. Don't we all.

NELL. He's just got to relocate. He's got a bungalow in Dymchurch.

WIN. And his wife says.

NELL. The lady wife wouldn't care to relocate. She's going through the change.

WIN. It's his funeral, don't waste your time.

NELL. I don't waste a lot.

WIN. Good weekend you?

NELL. You could say.

WIN. Which one?

NELL. One Friday, one Saturday.

WIN. Aye-aye. (p. 47–8)

Marlene is able to move between these codes which is the mark of her advancement. Mastering the language is a requirement for entry into any social group. If, in T. S. Eliot's phrase, you must 'prepare a face to meet the faces that you meet' you must also have command of the appropriate language. So Shona very quickly finds herself accepted when she is interviewed by Nell. She mirrors the new woman in confidence, attractiveness and ambition. She looks the part and echoes the speech and the sentiments.

NELL. You find it easy to get the initial interest do you?

SHONA. Oh yeh, I get plenty of initial interest.

NELL. And what about closing?

SHONA. I close, don't I?

NELL. Because that's what an employer is going to have doubts
    about . . . They think we listen to the buyer's doubts. They think
    we consider his needs and his feelings.

SHONA. I never consider people's feelings.

NELL. I was selling for six years, I can sell anything, I've sold in
    three continents, and I'm jolly as they come but I'm not very nice.

SHONA. I'm not very nice. (p. 61)

It follows that Nell can see Shona working in the office – 'there's
nothing officially going just now, but we're always on the lookout.
There's not that many of us. We could keep in touch.' Shona evidently
possesses, at least superficially, the characteristics of 'us'. Win has
sensed the same qualities in a client – 'Tough bird like us' – and Nell
says 'I always want the tough ones when I see them'. Shona's language,
however, lets her down eventually. Her description of a day's selling in
the North of England is a fantasy. It is a half-digested consumer's guide
to good living, full of clichés and unbelievable. Nell's response is the
more bitter because she has been deceived for so long. Shona's
education and experience have only partially equipped her for the new
materialist culture that she is anxious to enjoy. She cannot sustain the
image that her brazen confidence projects in her early, curt replies to
Nell. Likewise Jeanine's education has left her floundering. Her
limitations are exposed in the contrast between her linguistic ramblings
and Marlene's incisive questioning.

The questioning technique is frequently used as a method of
character definition. The three office interviews are each beautifully
shaped. Everything that we need to know about Jeanine, Louise and
Shona emerges clearly and each actor has plenty to work on to fill out
the character in performance. Marlene asks Jeanine sixteen questions in
as many lines and learns all she needs to know. Win asks Louise ten
penetrating questions which introduce her completely, and Nell asks
Shona twenty questions which do the same. When Angie visits the
office in Act Two both Marlene and Win ask her a lot of questions
which reveal as much about them as about Angie.

In *Top Girls* Churchill employs the original device of overlapping
dialogue. How this works is explained in the note to the layout of the
text on p. lvi. A speech usually follows the one immediately before it

but sometimes a speaker interrupts another, or continues speaking right through another's speech, or follows on from a speech earlier than the one preceding it. This occurs a lot in Act One and culminates in Act Three during the passionate argument between Marlene and Joyce when they are sometimes speaking at the same time. What is the purpose of this technique? It produced mixed reactions at first ('Overlapping dialogue is a brilliant technical feature' – Michael Coveney, 'an irritating conceit . . . which serves no purpose, real or symbolic' – Bryan Robertson). If an actor's words can't be heard it is easy to understand the frustration of an audience. However, the audience should be involved, not alienated. The 'speaking right through' or 'interruption' that occurs during the Act One dinner is the consequence of exuberance. The effect is partly one of surface naturalism. People excited at a party do speak at the same time. However, the dialogue is coherent and logical. The speakers hear what is said and respond to it. The audience is made to listen more acutely and is the more involved. They can also find the effect of the competing egos very funny. The language of Act One has a predominantly narrative purpose. Actors will find a distinctive 'voice' as they will a 'character' for the women of Act One, but the structure of their language is standard prose and although the dialogue is brilliantly orchestrated and witty the speech patterns are similar. Only Gret, with her monosyllabic interjections, is markedly different.

The overlapping in Act Three has a different purpose. The dramatist is able to simplify the argument, assuming the already informed make-up of the audience (a contemporary audience would bring their knowledge of the political argument *to* the play). What is shown in the row between the two sisters, now affected by the whisky they have drunk, is real personal distress. The overlapping dialogue helps to show the personal pain and damage that occurs to individuals as a direct consequence of political decisions that are made by others.

Language points to the fragmentation of British society and the survival of class distinctions when two 'groups' collide, which occurs with the intervention of Mrs Kidd in the office. Marlene introduces her to Angie:

> MRS KIDD. . . . I'm sorry if I'm interrupting your work. I know office work isn't housework / which is all interruptions.
> MARLENE. No, no, this is my niece. Angie. Mrs Kidd.

MRS KIDD. Very pleased to meet you.
ANGIE. Very well thank you. (p. 57)

Mrs Kidd replies with the conventional 'polite' response of her social group – 'Very pleased to meet you'. Angie, however, who might never have spoken before to a woman of Mrs Kidd's social background, responds disconcertedly to a question that hasn't been asked. Her 'Very well thank you' is the conditioned response to 'How are you?' But Angie is out of her depth, and it shows. Joyce is aware that Marlene mixes in a different social group. In a phrase of revealing awkwardness she is to admit 'You're ashamed of me if I came to your office, your smart friends, wouldn't you . . .' (p. 85)

The meeting between Marlene and Mrs Kidd is a confrontation of women from different backgrounds holding incompatible views about the role of women. There is an unconscious irony in Mrs Kidd's words 'you don't recognise me but we did meet, I remember you of course . . .' (p. 57). Marlene doesn't recognise her at first, but then she literally cannot understand why Mrs Kidd has come to the office, or what she is trying to say. As the truth dawns on her and she realises that Mrs Kidd has come to support her husband Marlene's response is forceful:

MRS KIDD. I had to do something.
MARLENE. Well you've done it, you've seen me. I think that's
    probably all we've time for. I'm sorry he's taking it out on you. He
    really is a shit, Howard. (p. 59)

The effect is shocking because of the word 'shit'. An English audience would know 'a shit' to be a vulgar term of contempt for somebody. But it is offensive. It is one of the words omitted from Partridge's *Smaller Slang Dictionary* 1976, because it is likely to offend 'against propriety or delicacy'. When Mrs Kidd loses control and echoes the distraught Howard – 'you're not natural' – Marlene tells her to 'piss off'. The phrase 'Could you please piss off' is controlled, but calculated to insult and to be effective. Angie thinks the use of this language by Marlene is 'wonderful' because she knows it is not acceptable in Mrs Kidd's social world. For Angie it implies a kind of triumph. In the theatre the response is likely to be complex. Mrs Kidd's request is unreasonable, but she is deeply upset and Marlene's response is impatient and even cruel. It reveals the extent of her hardness.

Just as the actor is responsible for finding the right voice and accent

for her character, so the text of *Top Girls* makes interpretative
demands on the actor to find the right meaning of a line. Meaning is
conveyed by stress and intonation. Many of the dialogues in the play
are made up of concise, very short sentences. This produces the sound
of natural speech in performance, but the emotional drive and
motivation has to be found by the actor. The text provides all the
evidence that is necessary.

Two examples should clarify how far the text has been constructed
for performance, and requires the actor to deliver the words
meaningfully. Towards the end of her interview Louise becomes
agitated and is advised by Win not to 'talk too much at an interview'.

> LOUISE. . . . . I only talk to you because it seems to me this is
>   different, it's your job to understand me, surely. You asked the
>   questions.
> WIN. I think I understand you sufficiently.
> LOUISE. Well good, that's good.
> WIN. Do you drink?
> LOUISE. Certainly not. I'm not a teetotaller, I think's that very
>   suspect, it's seen as being an alcoholic if you're teetotal . . . (p. 53)

The question is how should Win say 'Do you drink?' This depends on
how Win appears elsewhere in the play. 'Do you drink?' could be a
bitchy response. Win could have been upset during the interview by the
older woman defining the younger generation of executive, possibly
Win herself, as 'not so careful. They take themselves for granted'. A
further implied criticism could be seen in Louise's reply 'it's your job to
understand me, surely'. Win might respond unsympathetically with a
question that puts down Louise. It is obvious that Louise doesn't have
any fun in life, that she has no social pleasures. Why should Win take
criticism from her? However, in other scenes Win is shown to be
sensitive – much more so than Nell – and it is unlikely that she would
be unpleasant in this way. She treats Angie very sympathetically when
she finds her in the office, and in telling her own story she reveals both
strengths and weaknesses, intelligence and sensitivity:

> I like this better than sales, I'm not really that aggressive. I started
> thinking sales was a good job if you want to meet people, but you're
> meeting people that don't want to meet you. It's no good if you like

being liked. Here your clients want to meet you because you're the one doing them some good. They hope. (p. 65)

It is more likely that Win would be sympathetic to Louise, who is a very sad figure. She might sense that Louise drinks alcohol secretly and guiltily at home to cheer herself up. Win has done this – without the guilt – in her own past. She might want to encourage Louise towards a happier future, by erasing the guilt. The question 'Do you drink?' would then be asked with sympathetic understanding. The actor has to decide, and will do so in relation to the play as a whole. As it happens, Louise does not respond and Win doesn't pursue the point:

WIN. I drink.
LOUISE. I don't.
WIN. Good for you. (p. 53)

It is significant that Win should interview Louise and that Nell should interview Shona, given how they are presented and how they speak in the office at other times. Win, unlike Nell, is not jealous of Marlene's promotion.

Secondly, the ending shows how a deceptively simple vocabulary carries the potential for a very powerful emotional impact. When Marlene has been left alone by Joyce she 'sits wrapped in a blanket and has another drink. Angie comes in':

ANGIE. Mum?
MARLENE. Angie? What's the matter?
ANGIE. Mum?
MARLENE. No, she's gone to bed. It's Aunty Marlene.
ANGIE. Frightening.
MARLENE. Did you have a bad dream? . . . (p. 87)

A climax of emotional tension has been reached in the furious argument between Joyce and Marlene and this leaves a stillness and quietness in the theatre when Marlene is left alone on stage. Angie's entrance is poignant in the extreme. Angie, in distress, calls for her mother and Marlene – who is her mother – replies 'No, she's gone to bed. It's Aunty Marlene.' How is this to be spoken? An actor could project wretchedness and maternal guilt and draw audience sympathy towards her character. Marlene would be seen to be paying the cost of denying her own motherhood. Alternatively an actress could show that

Marlene has steeled herself to this rejection of Angie and consequently place the entire weight of audience sympathy onto Angie. However, the text allows for the weight of sympathy to be directed towards both characters. Marlene can show the cost of the rejection as it affects her, but still show that the rejection has been made, and that Angie has been left distraught. The playwright doesn't say *how* the words should be spoken. There is no adverbial advice. But the text is sufficiently complete for the actors to find the appropriate reading. Act Three is retrospective ('a year earlier') and the actress playing Marlene should see that without a conscious and deliberate choice concerning Angie, Marlene would not have progressed to being Managing Director of the 'Top Girls' agency – as we see her in Acts One and Two.

Structure

There is no precedent for the structure of *Top Girls*. As Caryl Churchill explained in an interview, she begins with 'content' and then finds the 'form'. 'You invent the rules, experiment all the time' (*Third Ear*, BBC Radio 3, 17.4.89). In the case of *Top Girls* the two predominant ideas were those of dead women coming back and women working. The settings of a restaurant and an employment agency are ideal for dramatising these subjects. However, inevitably, the originality of the concept proved disturbing to some. Rosalind Carne argued 'From a strictly mechanical point of view scene one is superfluous' (*Financial Times*) and Nicholas de Jong was also concerned about the first scene in relation to the rest – 'Churchill never really convinces that this dramatic backcloth to the play has any developed relationship or ironic contrast with what follows' (*Guardian*). The last Act being retroactive (a fact which 'emerges' during performance) also works against the convention of a forward moving plot where characters are affected by the action as it progresses.

Nevertheless the play does have a linear narrative, moving through Marlene's story and increasingly opening up the themes to a point where Marlene's decisions are fully revealed in relation to the present. There is a progressive and cumulative exposure of the female predicament which is explored around the character of Marlene, who invariably is the one character not doubled. The consequence of including a large number of characters in a play is to shift the focus from any one point of view, but Marlene's narrative, and her relationship with Joyce and Angie has a coherence by the end that has not been reduced by the sharp juxtaposition of earlier scenes.

Juxtaposition is a major structural device of *Top Girls*. Contrasting scenes and characters are set against each other and we in the audience are invited to make connections and distinctions. In the 'modern' scenes of the office and Joyce's house we are presented with contrasting images of modern Britain: the one urban, smart, affluent and optimistic, the other rural, static, poor and pessimistic. The combined effect is to suggest a fragmented society. The final image of the estranged Angie and Marlene brought together from these two worlds, is inconclusive. A climactic ending would be inappropriate for a play which emphasises problems of modern living. Angie and Joyce, as the play shows in Act Two, will continue to live in the real world. Max Stafford-Clark, writing to the dead author George Farquhar, suggests:

> We're a bit unused to happy endings in modern drama, George, they went out in the sixties. Nowadays we usually end plays on a melancholic note of elegant despair. It suits the political climate.
> (Letters to George, 1989)

The Play in Performance – How Many Actors?

To a feminist or socialist, indeed to any one concerned about the quality of modern life, the implications of *Top Girls* could be gloomy. 'Oh God, why are we all so miserable?' asks Marlene; 'Everyone's always crying in this house. Nobody takes any notice' says Joyce. However, in performance the play can be wonderfully exhilarating and positive in its effect. This is an apparent contradiction worth investigating.

Critical reaction was extremely enthusiastic about the first production of *Top Girls* at the Royal Court Theatre in 1982, directed by Max Stafford-Clark. The play was described as 'hugely entertaining' (*Sunday Express*) and the high quality of acting was particularly admired. The *Guardian* claimed 'There is no finer female playing in London than that achieved by these actresses' and that the play produced 'the most dynamic performances imaginable'. More specifically, for The *Spectator* the dramatist was magnificently served by 'the sharpest and most intelligent display of acting to be seen in London'. Very good acting is always compulsive and clearly the dramatic text offered a challenge that was relished by the original performers.

The actress Harriet Walter has written that the demands on actresses have traditionally been much less than on actors in the theatre. Women in plays have been regarded as simpler than men. In *Top Girls* actresses were offered, quite out of the norm, a variety of parts for women which were eloquent, witty, intelligent and unusual. Beyond this, most of the actors were able to play several roles, although this was not Churchill's original intention:

> For *Top Girls* at the Royal Court I wasn't thinking in terms of doubling at all. My original idea was to write a play for an enormous number of women, and I just wrote a play that had 16 women's parts in it. When it came to doing it, partly because it was being directed by Max Stafford-Clark who . . . is used to working and likes working in that way, partly financial considerations (I mean, no one's going to want to do a play with 16 actors when they can economise and do it with seven) and partly because it is obviously much more enjoyable for the actors and just for the whole *feel* of a play for it to be done by a company – it did seem to make a lot of sense to do it in that way. (Churchill, interviewed by Lynne Truss, in 'A Fair Cop' *Plays and Players* January 1984)

The 16 characters were performed by seven actors in the original production and subsequent productions have tended to follow suit. Only the actor playing Marlene was not involved in doubling. The doubling of characters isn't likely to be thematic in *Top Girls*. A direct link between characters would not be the intention. This can happen in the theatre – in Shakespeare's *A Midsummer Night's Dream* for example, where Theseus/Oberon and Hippolyta/Titania are sometimes doubled. In *Top Girls* doubling is more likely to be logical and functional. It could be based on appropriateness of physical appearance, or on the ability of an actor to make a costume change between scenes. It might even be based on a deliberate challenge to the audience's expectation of 'types'. The doubling and trebling of parts in the original production is not the only possible variation. The opportunity for women performers is stimulating and must be one of the reasons, along with the originality of the play, why it has been so popular abroad. *Top Girls* has been performed in over 20 countries. Good plays for women have been in high demand in the 1980s.

Doubling and trebling of parts can be exciting in the theatre as an exhibition of technique. It can also ensure that smaller parts are well played. It can, furthermore, contribute in performance to the meaning of a play. *Top Girls* questions the 'roles' that have been imposed on women, past and present. The doubling of parts by an actor can positively undermine the fixedness of roles. For example, Mrs Kidd and Joyce are from very different social backgrounds. As individuals they appear stuck in their social niche, limited and defined by it. When played by the same actress, as they were in the first production, the certainty of their predicament is open to question. As Act One shows that the past was different in many respects from the present, so the play implies the present might also be changed.

Further reading

Plays by Caryl Churchill

Plays: One, London: Methuen, 1985 (*Owners, Traps, Vinegar Tom, Light Shining in Buckinghamshire, Cloud Nine*)

Plays: Two, London: Methuen, 1990 (*Softcops, Top Girls, Fen, Serious Money*)

Plays: Three, London: Nick Hern Books, 1998 (*Ice Cream, Mad Forest, The Skriker, Thyestes, Lives of the Great Poisoners, A Mouthful of Birds*)

Churchill Shorts, London: Nick Hern Books, 1990 (*Abortive, The After-Dinner Joke, The Hospital at the Time of the Hot Fudge, Revealing the Judge's Wife, Lovesick, Three More Sleepless Nights, Schreber's Nervous Illness, Not Not Not Not Not Enough Oxygen*)

Light Shining in Buckinghamshire, London: Pluto Press, 1978; Nick Hern Books, 1989

Traps, London: Pluto Press, 1978; Nick Hern Books, 1989

Cloud Nine, London: Pluto Press, 1979; Nick Hern Books, 1989

Objections to Sex and Violence, published in *Plays by Women, Volume 4*, London: Methuen, 1985

Serious Money, London: Methuen, 1987; student edition, 2002

Ice Cream, London: Nick Hern Books, 1989

Mad Forest, London: Nick Hern Books, 1990

The Skriker, London: Nick Hern Books, 1994

Thyestes (a version of Seneca), London: Nick Hern Books, 1994

Blue Heart, London: Nick Hern Books, 1997

Hotel, London: Nick Hern Books, 1997

This Is a Chair, London: Nick Hern Books, 1999

Far Away, London: Nick Hern Books, 2000

A Number, London: Nick Hern Books, 2002

A Dream Play (adapted from Strindberg), London: Nick Hern Books, 2005

Drunk Enough To Say I Love You?, London: Nick Hern Books, 2006

Writing about Churchill

Elaine Aston, *Caryl Churchill*, Plymouth: Northcote House, 2nd edition, 2001

Sue-Ellen Case, *Feminism and Theatre*, London: Macmillan, 1988

Geraldine Cousin, Churchill's development (a study of) *Churchill: The Playwright*, London: Methuen, 1989

Linda Fitzsimmons, *File on Churchill*, London: Methuen, 1989 (a most useful companion which contains critical reactions to productions of her work, comments of the playwright, and a good bibliography including the many articles written on Churchill)

Amelia Howe Kritzer, *The Plays of Caryl Churchill: Theatre of Empowerment*, London and Baskingstoke: Macmillan, 1991

Sheila Rabillard (ed.), *Essays on Caryl Churchill: Contemporary Representations,* Winnipeg: Blizzard, 2001

Phyllis R. Randall (ed.), *Caryl Churchill: A Casebook*, London and New York: Garland, 1988

Victoria D. Sullivan, *Caryl Churchill*, New York: Scribner's, 1997

Michelene Wandor, *Look back in Gender: Sexuality and the Family in Post-War British Drama,* London: Methuen, 1987

TOP GIRLS

Note on characters

ISABELLA BIRD (1831-1904) lived in Edinburgh, travelled extensively between the ages of 40 and 70.

LADY NIJO (b.1258) Japanese, was an Emperor's courtesan and later a Buddhist nun who travelled on foot through Japan.

DULL GRET is the subject of the Brueghel painting, Dulle Griet, in which a woman in an apron and armour leads a crowd of women charging through hell and fighting the devils.

POPE JOAN, disguised as a man, is thought to have been Pope between 854-856.

PATIENT GRISELDA is the obedient wife whose story is told by Chaucer in The Clerk's Tale of *The Canterbury Tales*.

Note on layout

A speech usually follows the one immediately before it BUT:
1: when one character starts speaking before the other has finished, the point of interruption is marked / .

eg. ISABELLA:	This is the Emperor of Japan? / I once met the Emperor of Morocco.
NIJO:	In fact he was the ex-Emperor.

2: a character sometimes continues speaking right through another's speech:

eg. ISABELLA:	When I was forty I thought my life was over. / Oh I was pitiful. I was
NIJO:	I didn't say I felt it for twenty years. Not every minute.
ISABELLA:	sent on a cruise for my health and I felt even worse. Pains in my bones, pins and needles . . . etc.

3: sometimes a speech follows on from a speech earlier than the one immediately before it, and continuity is marked*.

eg. GRISELDA:	I'd seen him riding by, we all had. And he'd seen me in the fields with the sheep*.
ISABELLA:	I would have been well suited to minding sheep.
NIJO:	And Mr Nugent riding by.
ISABELLA:	Of course not, Nijo, I mean a healthy life in the open air.
JOAN:	*He just rode up while you were minding the sheep and asked you to marry him?

where 'in the fields with the sheep' is the cue to both 'I would have been' and 'He just rode up'.

Top Girls was first performed at the Royal Court Theatre, London on 28 August 1982 with the following cast:

MARLENE	Gwen Taylor
ISABELLA BIRD JOYCE MRS KIDD	Deborah Findlay
LADY NIJO WIN	Lindsay Duncan
DULL GRET ANGIE	Carole Hayman
POPE JOAN LOUISE	Selina Cadell
PATIENT GRISELDA NELL JEANINE	Lesley Manville
WAITRESS KIT SHONA	Lou Wakefield

Directed by Max Stafford Clark
Designed by Peter Hartwell

This production transferred to Joe Papp's Public Theatre, New York, later the same year, and returned to the Royal Court early in 1983.

ACT ONE	Restaurant. Saturday night.
ACT TWO	
Scene One:	'Top Girls' Employment agency. Monday morning.
Scene Two:	Joyce's back yard. Sunday afternoon.
Scene Three:	Employment agency. Monday morning.
ACT THREE	Joyce's kitchen. Sunday evening, a year earlier.

Production note
Top Girls was originally written in three acts and I still find
that structure clearer: Act One, the dinner; Act Two, Angie's
story; Act Three, the year before. But two intervals do hold
things up, so in the original production we made it two acts
with the interval after what is here Act Two, scene two. Do
whichever you prefer.

Caryl Churchill *1985*

Note
The 1985 New Cross Theatre, London production was directed by
Nesta Jones and designed by Gerald Lidstone.

Carole Hayman as Dull Gret in the 1982 Royal Court, London
production. Photo © Catherine Ashmore.

l. to r.: Carole Hayman as Dull Gret, Lindsay Duncan as Lady Nijo, Gwen Taylor as Marlene, Selina Cadell as Pope Joan, Lou Wakefield as Waitress (standing), Lesley Manville as Patient Griselda and Deborah Findlay as Isabella Bird in the 1982 Royal Court, London production. Photo © Catherine Ashmore.

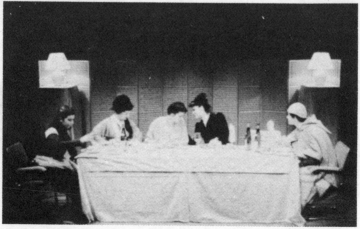

l. to r.: Nicola Hollinshead as Dull Gret, Nancy McClean as Lady Nijo, Patricia Phoenix as Marlene, Emma Healey as Isabella Bird and Helene Zumbrunn as Pope Joan in the 1985 New Cross Theatre, London production. Photo © Tony Nandi.

l. to r.: Carole Hayman as Angie and Gwen Taylor as Marlene in the 1982 Royal Court, London production. Photo © Catherine Ashmore.

l. to r.: Patricia Phoenix as Marlene and Nicola Hollinshead as Jeanine in the 1985 New Cross Theatre, London production. Photo © Tony Nandi.

l. to r.: Deborah Findlay as Joyce and Gwen Taylor as Marlene in the 1982 Royal Court, London production. Photo © Catherine Ashmore.

l. to r.: Patricia Phoenix as Marlene, Emma Healey as Joyce and Sally Poplar as Angie in the 1985 New Cross Theatre, London production. Photo © Tony Nandi.

ACT ONE

Restaurant. Table set for dinner with white tablecloth. Six places.
MARLENE *and* WAITRESS.

MARLENE. Excellent, yes, table for six. One of them's going to
be late but we won't wait. I'd like a bottle of Frascati straight
away if you've got one really cold.

The WAITRESS *goes.*

ISABELLA BIRD *arrives.*

Here we are. Isabella.

ISABELLA. Congratulations, my dear.

MARLENE. Well, it's a step. It makes for a party. I haven't time
for a holiday. I'd like to go somewhere exotic like you but I
can't get away. I don't know how you could bear to leave
Hawaii. / I'd like to lie in the sun forever, except of course I

ISABELLA. I did think of settling.

MARLENE. can't bear sitting still.

ISABELLA. I sent for my sister Hennie to come and join me. I
said, Hennie we'll live here forever and help the natives. You
can buy two sirloins of beef for what a pound of chops costs
in Edinburgh. And Hennie wrote back, the dear, that yes, she
would come to Hawaii if I wished, but I said she had far better
stay where she was. Hennie was suited to life in Tobermory.

MARLENE. Poor Hennie.

ISABELLA. Do you have a sister?

MARLENE. Yes in fact.

ISABELLA. Hennie was happy. She was good. I did miss its face, my own pet. But I couldn't stay in Scotland. I loathed the constant murk.

MARLENE. Ah! Nijo!

She sees LADY NIJO *arrive.*

The WAITRESS *enters with wine.*

NIJO. Marlene!

MARLENE. I think a drink while we wait for the others. I think a drink anyway. What a week.

The WAITRESS *pours wine.*

NIJO. It was always the men who used to get so drunk. I'd be one of the maidens, passing the sake.

ISABELLA. I've had sake. Small hot drink. Quite fortifying after a day in the wet.

NIJO. One night my father proposed three rounds of three cups, which was normal, and then the Emperor should have said three rounds of three cups, but he said three rounds of nine cups, so you can imagine. Then the Emperor passed his sake cup to my father and said, 'Let the wild goose come to me this spring.'

MARLENE. Let the what?

NIJO. It's a literary allusion to a tenth-century epic, / His Majesty was very cultured.

ISABELLA: This is the Emperor of Japan? / I once met the Emperor of Morocco.

NIJO. In fact he was the ex-Emperor.

MARLENE. But he wasn't old? / Did you, Isabella?

NIJO. Twenty-nine.

ISABELLA. Oh it's a long story.

MARLENE. Twenty-nine's an excellent age.

NIJO. Well I was only fourteen and I knew he meant something but I didn't know what. He sent me an eight-layered gown and I sent it back. So when the time came I did nothing but cry. My thin gowns were badly ripped. But even that morning when he left / – he'd a green robe with a scarlet lining and

MARLENE. Are you saying he raped you?

NIJO. very heavily embroidered trousers, I already felt different about him. It made me uneasy. No, of course not, Marlene, I belonged to him, it was what I was brought up for from a baby. I soon found I was sad if he stayed away. It was depressing day after day not knowing when he would come. I never enjoyed taking other women to him.

ISABELLA. I certainly never saw my father drunk. He was a clergyman. / And I didn't get married till I was fifty.

The WAITRESS *brings menus.*

NIJO. Oh, my father was a very religious man. Just before he died he said to me, 'Serve His Majesty, be respectful, if you lose his favour enter holy orders.'

MARLENE. But he meant stay in a convent, not go wandering round the country.

NIJO. Priests were often vagrants, so why not a nun? You think I shouldn't? /I still did what my father wanted.

MARLENE. No no, I think you should. / I think it was wonderful.

DULL GRET *arrives.*

ISABELLA. I tried to do what my father wanted.

MARLENE. Gret, good. Nijo. Gret. / I know Griselda's going to be late, but should we wait for Joan? / Let's get you a drink.

ISABELLA. Hello Gret! (*Continues to* NIJO:) I tried to be a clergyman's daughter. Needlework, music, charitable schemes. I had a tumour removed from my spine and spent a great deal of time on the sofa. I studied the metaphysical poets and hymnology. / I thought I enjoyed intellectual pursuits.

NIJO. Ah, you like poetry. I come of a line of eight generations of poets. Father had a poem / in the anthology.

ISABELLA. My father taught me Latin although I was a girl. / But

MARLENE. They didn't have Latin at my school.

ISABELLA. really I was more suited to manual work. Cooking, washing, mending, riding horses. / Better than reading books,

NIJO. Oh but I'm sure you're very clever.

ISABELLA. eh Gret? A rough life in the open air.

NIJO. I can't say I enjoyed my rough life. What I enjoyed most was being the Emperor's favourite / and wearing thin silk.

ISABELLA: Did you have any horses, Gret?

GRET. Pig.

POPE JOAN *arrives.*

MARLENE. Oh Joan, thank God, we can order. Do you know everyone? We were just talking about learning Latin and being clever girls. Joan was by way of an infant prodigy. Of course you were. What excited you when you were ten?

JOAN. Because angels are without matter they are not individuals. Every angel is a species.

MARLENE. There you are.

They laugh. They look at menus.

ISABELLA. Yes, I forgot all my Latin. But my father was the mainspring of my life and when he died I was so grieved. I'll have the chicken, please, / and the soup.

NIJO. Of course you were grieved. My father was saying his prayers and he dozed off in the sun. So I touched his knee to rouse him. 'I wonder what will happen,' he said, and then he was dead before he finished the sentence. / If he'd died saying

MARLENE. What a shock.

NIJO. his prayers he would have gone straight to heaven. / Waldorf salad.

JOAN. Death is the return of all creatures to God.

NIJO. I shouldn't have woken him.

JOAN. Damnation only means ignorance of the truth. I was always attracted by the teachings of John the Scot, though he was inclined to confuse / God and the world.

ISABELLA. Grief always overwhelmed me at the time.

MARLENE. What I fancy is a rare steak. Gret?

ISABELLA. I am of course a member of the / Church of England.*

GRET. Potatoes.

MARLENE. *I haven't been to church for years. / I like Christmas carols.

ISABELLA. Good works matter more than church attendance.

MARLENE. Make that two steaks and a lot of potatoes. Rare. But I don't do good works either.

JOAN. Canelloni, please, / and a salad.

ISABELLA. Well, I tried, but oh dear. Hennie did good works.

NIJO. The first half of my life was all sin and the second / all repentance.*

MARLENE. Oh what about starters?

GRET. Soup.

JOAN. *And which did you like best?

MARLENE. Were your travels just a penance? Avocado vinaigrette. Didn't you / enjoy yourself?

JOAN. Nothing to start with for me, thank you.

NIJO. Yes, but I was very unhappy. / It hurt to remember

MARLENE. And the wine list.

NIJO. the past. I think that was repentance.

MARLENE. Well I wonder.

NIJO. I might have just been homesick.

MARLENE. Or angry.

NIJO. Not angry, no, / why angry?

GRET. Can we have some more bread?

MARLENE. Don't you get angry? I get angry.

NIJO. But what about?

MARLENE. Yes let's have two more Frascati. And some more bread, please.

The WAITRESS *exits.*

ISABELLA. I tried to understand Buddhism when I was in Japan but all this birth and death succeeding each other through eternities just filled me with the most profound melancholy. I do like something more active.

NIJO. You couldn't say I was inactive. I walked every day for twenty years.

ISABELLA. I don't mean walking. / I mean in the head.

NIJO. I vowed to copy five Mahayana sutras. / Do you know how

MARLENE. I don't think religious beliefs are something we have in common. Activity yes.

NIJO. long they are? My head was active. / My head ached.

JOAN. It's no good being active in heresy.

ISABELLA. What heresy? She's calling the Church of England / a heresy.

JOAN. There are some very attractive / heresies.

NIJO. I had never heard of Christianity. Never / heard of it. Barbarians.

MARLENE. Well I'm not a Christian. / And I'm not a Buddhist.

ISABELLA. You have heard of it?

MARLENE. We don't all have to believe the same.

ISABELLA. I knew coming to dinner with a pope we should keep off religion.

JOAN. I always enjoy a theological argument. But I won't try to convert you, I'm not a missionary. Anyway I'm a heresy myself

ISABELLA. There are some barbaric practices in the east.

NIJO. Barbaric?

ISABELLA. Among the lower classes.

NIJO. I wouldn't know.

ISABELLA. Well theology always made my head ache.

MARLENE. Oh good, some food.

WAITRESS *is bringing the first course.*

NIJO. How else could I have left the court if I wasn't a nun?
When father died I had only His Majesty. So when I fell out of
favour I had nothing. Religion is a kind of nothing / and I
dedicated what was left of me to nothing.

ISABELLA. That's what I mean about Buddhism. It doesn't brace.

MARLENE. Come on, Nijo, have some wine.

NIJO. Haven't you ever felt like that? Nothing will ever happen
again. I am dead already. You've all felt / like that.

ISABELLA. You thought your life was over but it wasn't.

JOAN. You wish it was over.

GRET. Sad.

MARLENE. Yes, when I first came to London I sometimes . . .
and when I got back from America I did. But only for a few
hours. Not twenty years.

ISABELLA. When I was forty I thought my life was over. / Oh I

NIJO. I didn't say I felt it for twenty years. Not every minute.

ISABELLA. was pitiful. I was sent on a cruise for my health and I
felt even worse. Pains in my bones, pins and needles in my
hands, swelling behind the ears, and — oh, stupidity. I shook
all over, indefinable terror. And Australia seemed to me a
hideous country, the acacias stank like drains. / I had a

NIJO. You were homesick.

ISABELLA. photograph for Hennie but I told her I wouldn't
send it, my hair had fallen out and my clothes were crooked, I
looked completely insane and suicidal.

NIJO. So did I, exactly, dressed as a nun. I was wearing walking
shoes for the first time.

ISABELLA. I longed to go home, / but home to what? Houses

NIJO. I longed to go back ten years.

ISABELLA. are so perfectly dismal.

MARLENE. I thought travelling cheered you both up.

ISABELLA. Oh it did / of course. It was on the trip from

NIJO. I'm not a cheerful person, Marlene. I just laugh a lot.

ISABELLA. Australia to the Sandwich Isles, I fell in love with the sea. There were rats in the cabin and ants in the food but suddenly it was like a new world. I woke up every morning happy, knowing there would be nothing to annoy me. No nervousness. No dressing.

NIJO. Don't you like getting dressed? I adored my clothes. / When I was chosen to give sake to His Majesty's brother,

MARLENE. You had prettier colours than Isabella.

NIJO. the Emperor Kameyana, on his formal visit, I wore raw silk pleated trousers and a seven-layered gown in shades of red, and two outer garments, / yellow lined with green and a light

MARLENE. Yes, all that silk must have been very . . .

The WAITRESS *starts to clear the first course.*

JOAN. I dressed as a boy when I left home.*

NIJO. green jacket. Lady Betto had a five-layered gown in shades of green and purple.

ISABELLA. *You dressed as a boy?

MARLENE. Of course, / for safety.

JOAN. It was easy, I was only twelve. Also women weren't / allowed in the library. We wanted to study in Athens.

MARLENE. You ran away alone?

JOAN. No, not alone, I went with my friend. / He was sixteen

NIJO. Ah, an elopement.

JOAN. but I thought I knew more science than he did and almost as much philosophy.

ISABELLA. Well I always travelled as a lady and I repudiated strongly any suggestion in the press that I was other than feminine.

MARLENE. I don't wear trousers in the office. / I could but I don't

ISABELLA. There was no great danger to a woman of my age and appearance.

MARLENE. And you got away with it, Joan?

JOAN. I did then.

The WAITRESS *starts to bring the main course.*

MARLENE. And nobody noticed anything?

JOAN. They noticed I was a very clever boy. / And when I

MARLENE. I couldn't have kept pretending for so long.

JOAN. shared a bed with my friend, that was ordinary — two poor students in a lodging house. I think I forgot I was pretending.

ISABELLA. Rocky Mountain Jim, Mr Nugent, showed me no disrespect. He found it interesting, I think, that I could make scones and also lasso cattle. Indeed he declared his love for me, which was most distressing.

NIJO. What did he say? / We always sent poems first.

MARLENE. What did you say?

ISABELLA. I urged him to give up whisky, / but he said it was too late.

MARLENE. Oh Isabella.

ISABELLA. He had lived alone in the mountains for many years.

MARLENE. But did you — ?

The WAITRESS *goes.*

ISABELLA. Mr Nugent was a man that any woman might love but none could marry. I came back to England.

NIJO. Did you write him a poem when you left? / Snow on the

MARLENE. Did you never see him again?

ISABELLA. No, never.

NIJO. mountains. My sleeves are wet with tears. In England no tears, no snow.

ISABELLA. Well, I say never. One morning very early in Switzerland, it was a year later, I had a vision of him as I last saw him / in his trapper's clothes with his hair round his face,

NIJO. A ghost!

ISABELLA. and that was the day, / I learnt later, he died with a

NIJO. Ah!

ISABELLA. bullet in his brain. / He just bowed to me and vanished.

MARLENE. Oh Isabella.

NIJO. When your lover dies — One of my lovers died. / The priest Ariake.

JOAN. My friend died. Have we all got dead lovers?

MARLENE. Not me, sorry.

NIJO (*to* ISABELLA). I wasn't a nun, I was still at court, but he was a priest, and when he came to me he dedicated his whole life to hell. / He knew that when he died he would fall into one of the three lower realms. And he died, he did die.

JOAN (*to* MARLENE). I'd quarrelled with him over the teachings of John the Scot, who held that our ignorance of God is the same as his ignorance of himself. He only knows what he creates because he creates everything he knows but he himself is above being — do you follow?

MARLENE. No, but go on.

NIJO. I couldn't bear to think / in what shape would he be reborn.*

JOAN. St. Augustine maintained that the Neo-Platonic Ideas are indivisible from God, but I agreed with John that the created

ISABELLA. *Buddhism is really most uncomfortable.

JOAN. world is essences derived from Ideas which derived from God. As Denys the Areopagite said — the pseudo-Denys — first we give God a name, then deny it / then reconcile the

NIJO. In what shape would he return?

JOAN contradiction by looking beyond / those terms —

MARLENE. Sorry, what? Denys said what?

JOAN. Well we disagreed about it, we quarrelled. And next day he was ill, /I was so annoyed with him, all the time I was

NIJO. Misery in this life and worse in the next, all because of me.

JOAN. nursing him I kept going over the arguments in my mind. Matter is not a means of knowing the essence. The source of the species is the Idea. But then I realised he'd never understand my arguments again, and that night he died. John the Scot held that the individual disintegrates / and there is no personal immortality.

ISABELLA. I wouldn't have you think I was in love with Jim Nugent. It was yearning to save him that I felt.

MARLENE (*to* JOAN). So what did you do?

JOAN. First I decided to stay a man. I was used to it. And I wanted to devote my life to learning. Do you know why I went to Rome? Italian men didn't have beards.

ISABELLA. The loves of my life were Hennie, my own pet, and my dear husband the doctor, who nursed Hennie in her last illness. I knew it would be terrible when Hennie died but I didn't know how terrible. I felt half of myself had gone. How could I go on my travels without that sweet soul waiting at home for my letters? It was Doctor Bishop's devotion to her in her last illness that made me decide to marry him. He and Hennie had the same sweet character. I had not.

NIJO. I thought his majesty had sweet character because when he found out about Ariake he was so kind. But really it was because he no longer cared for me. One night he even sent me out to a man who had been pursuing me. /He lay awake on the other side of the screens and listened.

ISABELLA. I did wish marriage had seemed more of a step. I tried very hard to cope with the ordinary drudgery of life. I was ill again with carbuncles on the spine and nervous prostration. I ordered a tricycle, that was my idea of adventure then. And John himself fell ill, with erysipelas and anaemia. I began to love him with my whole heart but it was too late. He was a skeleton with transparent white hands. I wheeled him on various seafronts in a bathchair. And he faded and left me. There was nothing in my life. The doctors said I had gout /

and my heart was much affected.

NIJO. There was nothing in my life, nothing, without the Emperor's favour. The Empress had always been my enemy, Marlene, she said I had no right to wear three-layered gowns. / But I was the adopted daughter of my grandfather the Prime Minister. I had been publicly granted permission to wear thin silk.

JOAN. There was nothing in my life except my studies. I was obsessed with pursuit of the truth. I taught at the Greek School in Rome, which St Augustine had made famous. I was poor, I worked hard. I spoke apparently brilliantly, I was still very young, I was a stranger; suddenly I was quite famous, I was everyone's favourite. Huge crowds came to hear me. The day after they made me cardinal I fell ill and lay two weeks without speaking, full of terror and regret. / But then I got up

MARLENE. Yes, success is very . . .

JOAN. determined to go on. I was seized again / with a desperate longing for the absolute.

ISABELLA. Yes, yes, to go on. I sat in Tobermory among Hennie's flowers and sewed a complete outfit in Jaeger flannel. / I was fifty-six years old.

NIJO. Out of favour but I didn't die. I left on foot, nobody saw me go. For the next twenty years I walked through Japan.

GRET. Walking is good.

The WAITRESS *enters.*

JOAN. Pope Leo died and I was chosen. All right then. I would be Pope. I would know God. I would know everything.

ISABELLA. I determined to leave my grief behind and set off for Tibet.

MARLENE. Magnificent all of you. We need some more wine, please, two bottles I think, Griselda isn't even here yet, and I want to drink a toast to you all.

ISABELLA. To yourself surely, / we're here to celebrate your success.

NIJO. Yes, Marlene.

JOAN. Yes, what is it exactly, Marlene?

MARLENE. Well it's not Pope but it is managing director.*

JOAN. And you find work for people.

MARLENE. Yes, an employment agency.

NIJO. *Over all the women you work with. And the men.

ISABELLA. And very well deserved too. I'm sure it's just the beginning of something extraordinary.

MARLENE. Well it's worth a party.

ISABELLA. To Marlene.*

MARLENE. And all of us.

JOAN. *Marlene.

NIJO. Marlene.

GRET. Marlene.

MARLENE. We've all come a long way. To our courage and the way we changed our lives and our extraordinary achievements.

They laugh and drink a toast.

ISABELLA. Such adventures. We were crossing a mountain pass at seven thousand feet, the cook was all to pieces, the muleteers suffered fever and snow blindness. But even though my spine was agony I managed very well.

MARLENE. Wonderful.

NIJO. Once I was ill for four months lying alone at an inn. Nobody to offer a horse to Buddha. I had to live for myself, and I did live.

ISABELLA. Of course you did. It was far worse returning to Tobermory. I always felt dull when I was stationary. / That's why I could never stay anywhere.

NIJO. Yes, that's it exactly. New sights. The shrine by the beach, the moon shining on the sea. The goddess had vowed to save all living things. /She would even save the fishes. I was full of hope.

JOAN. I had thought the Pope would know everything. I thought God would speak to me directly. But of course he knew I was a woman.

MARLENE. But nobody else even suspected?

The WAITRESS *brings more wine.*

JOAN. In the end I did take a lover again.*

ISABELLA. In the Vatican?

GRET. *Keep you warm.

NIJO. *Ah, lover.

MARLENE. *Good for you.

JOAN. He was one of my chamberlains. There are such a lot of servants when you're a Pope. The food's very good. And I realised I did know the truth. Because whatever the Pope says, that's true.

NIJO. What was he like, the chamberlain?*

GRET. Big cock.

ISABELLA. Oh Gret.

MARLENE. *Did he fancy you when he thought you were a fella?

NIJO. What was he like?

JOAN. He could keep a secret.

MARLENE. So you did know everything.

JOAN. Yes, I enjoyed being Pope. I consecrated bishops and let people kiss my feet. I received the King of England when he came to submit to the church. Unfortunately there were earthquakes, and some village reported it had rained blood, and in France there was a plague of giant grasshoppers, but I don't think that can have been my fault, do you?*

Laughter.

The grasshoppers fell on the English Channel and were

washed up on shore and their bodies rotted and poisoned the air and everyone in those parts died.

Laughter.

ISABELLA. *Such superstition! I was nearly murdered in China by a howling mob. They thought the barbarians ate babies and put them under railway sleepers to make the tracks steady, and ground up their eyes to make the lenses of cameras. / So

MARLENE. And you had a camera!

ISABELLA. they were shouting, 'child-eater, child-eater.' Some people tried to sell girl babies to Europeans for cameras or stew!

Laughter.

MARLENE. So apart from the grasshoppers it was a great success.

JOAN. Yes, if it hadn't been for the baby I expect I'd have lived to an old age like Theodora of Alexandria, who lived as a monk. She was accused by a girl / who fell in love with her of being the father of her child and –

NIJO. But tell us what happened to your baby. I had some babies.

MARLENE. Didn't you think of getting rid of it?

JOAN. Wouldn't that be a worse sin than having it? / But a Pope with a child was about as bad as possible.

MARLENE. I don't know, you're the Pope.

JOAN. But I wouldn't have known how to get rid of it.

MARLENE. Other Popes had children, surely.

JOAN. They didn't give birth to them.

NIJO. Well you were a woman.

JOAN. Exactly and I shouldn't have been a woman. Women, children and lunatics can't be Pope.

MARLENE. So the only thing to do / was to get rid of it somehow.

NIJO. You had to have it adopted secretly.

JOAN. But I didn't know what was happening. I thought I was getting fatter, but then I was eating more and sitting about, the life of a Pope is quite luxurious. I don't think I'd spoken to a woman since I was twelve. The chamberlain was the one who realised.

MARLENE. And by then it was too late.

JOAN. Oh I didn't want to pay attention. It was easier to do nothing.

NIJO. But you had to plan for having it. You had to say you were ill and go away.

JOAN. That's what I should have done I suppose.

MARLENE. Did you want them to find out?

NIJO. I too was often in embarrassing situations, there's no need for a scandal. My first child was His Majesty's, which unfortunately died, but my second was Akebono's. I was seventeen. He was in love with me when I was thirteen, he was very upset when I had to go to the Emperor, it was very romantic, a lot of poems. Now His Majesty hadn't been near me for two months so he thought I was four months pregnant when I was really six, so when I reached the ninth month / I

JOAN. I never knew what month it was.

NIJO. announced I was seriously ill, and Akebono announced he had gone on a religious retreat. He held me round the waist and lifted me up as the baby was born. He cut the cord with a short sword, wrapped the baby in white and took it away. It was only a girl but I was sorry to lose it. Then I told the Emperor that the baby had miscarried because of my illness, and there you are. The danger was past.

JOAN. But Nijo, I wasn't used to having a woman's body.

ISABELLA. So what happened?

JOAN. I didn't know of course that it was near the time. It was Rogation Day, there was always a procession. I was on the horse dressed in my robes and a cross was carried in front of me, and all the cardinals were following, and all the clergy of Rome, and a huge crowd of people. / We set off from

MARLENE. Total Pope.

JOAN. St Peter's to go to St John's. I had felt a slight pain earlier, I thought it was something I'd eaten, and then it came back, and came back more often. I thought when this is over I'll go to bed. There were still long gaps when I felt perfectly all right and I didn't want to attract attention to myself and spoil the ceremony. Then I suddenly realised what it must be. I had to last out till I could get home and hide. Then something changed, my breath started to catch, I couldn't plan things properly any more. We were in a little street that goes between St Clement's and the Colosseum, and I just had to get off the horse and sit down for a minute. Great waves of pressure were going through my body, I heard sounds like a cow lowing, they came out of my mouth. Far away I heard people screaming, 'The Pope is ill, the Pope is dying.' And the baby just slid out onto the road.*

MARLENE. The cardinals / won't have known where to put themselves.

NIJO. Oh dear, Joan, what a thing to do! In the street!

ISABELLA. *How embarrassing.

GRET. In a field, yah.

They are laughing.

JOAN. One of the cardinals said, 'The Antichrist!' and fell over in a faint.

They all laugh.

MARLENE. So what did they do? They weren't best pleased.

JOAN. They took me by the feet and dragged me out of town and stoned me to death.

They stop laughing.

MARLENE. Joan, how horrible.

JOAN. I don't really remember.

NIJO. And the child died too?

JOAN. Oh yes, I think so, yes.

Pause.

The WAITRESS *enters to clear the plates. They start talking quietly.*

ISABELLA (*to* JOAN). I never had any children. I was very fond of horses.

NIJO (*to* MARLENE). I saw my daughter once. She was three years old. She wore a plum-red / small-sleeved gown. Akebono's

ISABELLA. Birdie was my favourite. A little Indian bay mare I rode in the Rocky Mountains.

NIJO. wife had taken the child because her own died. Everyone thought I was just a visitor. She was being brought up carefully so she could be sent to the palace like I was.

ISABELLA. Legs of iron and always cheerful, and such a pretty face. If a stranger led her she reared up like a bronco.

NIJO. I never saw my third child after he was born, the son of Ariake the priest. Ariake held him on his lap the day he was born and talked to him as if he could understand, and cried. My fourth child was Ariake's too. Ariake died before he was born. I didn't want to see anyone, I stayed alone in the hills. It was a boy again, my third son. But oddly enough I felt nothing for him.

MARLENE. How many children did you have, Gret?

GRET. Ten.

ISABELLA. Whenever I came back to England I felt I had so much to atone for. Hennie and John were so good. I did no good in my life. I spent years in self-gratification. So I hurled myself into committees, I nursed the people of Tobermory in the epidemic of influenza, I lectured the Young Women's Christian Association on Thrift. I talked and talked explaining how the East was corrupt and vicious. My travels must do good to someone beside myself. I wore myself out with good causes.

MARLENE. Oh God, why are we all so miserable?

JOAN. The procession never went down that street again.

MARLENE. They rerouted it specially?

JOAN. Yes they had to go all round to avoid it. And they introduced a pierced chair.

MARLENE. A pierced chair?

JOAN. Yes, a chair made out of solid marble with a hole in the seat / and it was in the Chapel of the Saviour, and after he was

MARLENE. You're not serious.

JOAN. elected the Pope had to sit in it.

MARLENE. And someone looked up his skirts? / Not really?

ISABELLA. What an extraordinary thing.

JOAN. Two of the clergy / made sure he was a man.

NIJO. On their hands and knees!

MARLENE. A pierced chair!

GRET. Balls!

GRISELDA *arrives unnoticed.*

NIJO. Why couldn't he just pull up his robe?

JOAN. He had to sit there and look dignified.

MARLENE. You could have made all your chamberlains sit in it.*

GRET. Big one, small one.

NIJO. Very useful chair at court.

ISABELLA. *Or the laird of Tobermory in his kilt.

They are quite drunk. They get the giggles.

MARLENE *notices* GRISELDA.

MARLENE. Griselda! / There you are. Do you want to eat?

GRISELDA. I'm sorry I'm so late. No, no, don't bother.

MARLENE. Of course it's no bother. / Have you eaten?

GRISELDA. No really, I'm not hungry.

MARLENE. Well have some pudding.

GRISELDA. I never eat pudding.

MARLENE. Griselda, I hope you're not anorexic. We're having pudding, I am, and getting nice and fat.

GRISELDA. Oh if everyone is. I don't mind.

MARLENE. Now who do you know? This is Joan who was Pope in the ninth century, and Isabella Bird, the Victorian traveller, and Lady Nijo from Japan, Emperor's concubine and Buddhist nun, thirteenth century, nearer your own time, and Gret who was painted by Brueghel. Griselda's in Boccaccio and Petrarch and Chaucer because of her extraordinary marriage. I'd like profiteroles because they're disgusting.

JOAN. Zabaglione, please.

ISABELLA. Apple pie / and cream.

NIJO. What's this?

MARLENE. Zabaglione, it's Italian, it's what Joan's having, / it's delicious.

NIJO. A Roman Catholic / dessert? Yes please.

MARLENE. Gret?

GRET. Cake.

GRISELDA. Just cheese and biscuits, thank you.

MARLENE. Yes, Griselda's life is like a fairy-story, except it starts with marrying the prince.

GRISELDA. He's only a marquis, Marlene.

MARLENE. Well everyone for miles around is his liege and he's absolute lord of life and death and you were the poor but beautiful peasant girl and he whisked you off. / Near enough a prince.

NIJO. How old were you?

GRISELDA. Fifteen.

NIJO. I was brought up in court circles and it was still a shock. Had you ever seen him before?

GRISELDA. I'd seen him riding by, we all had. And he'd seen me in the fields with the sheep.*

ISABELLA. I would have been well suited to minding sheep.

NIJO. And Mr Nugent riding by.

ISABELLA. Of course not, Nijo, I mean a healthy life in the open air.

JOAN. *He just rode up while you were minding the sheep and asked you to marry him?

GRISELDA. No, no, it was on the wedding day. I was waiting outside the door to see the procession. Everyone wanted him to get married so there'd be an heir to look after us when he died, / and at last he announced a day for the wedding but

MARLENE. I don't think Walter wanted to get married. It is Walter? Yes.

GRISELDA. nobody knew who the bride was, we thought it must be a foreign princess, we were longing to see her. Then the carriage stopped outside our cottage and we couldn't see the bride anywhere. And he came and spoke to my father.

NIJO. And your father told you to serve the Prince.

GRISELDA. My father could hardly speak. The Marquis said it wasn't an order, I could say no, but if I said yes I must always obey him in everything.

MARLENE. That's when you should have suspected.

GRISELDA. But of course a wife must obey her husband. / And of course I must obey the Marquis.*

ISABELLA. I swore to obey dear John, of course, but it didn't seem to arise. Naturally I wouldn't have wanted to go abroad while I was married.

MARLENE. *Then why bother to mention it at all? He'd got a thing about it, that's why.

GRISELDA. I'd rather obey the Marquis than a boy from the village.

MARLENE. Yes, that's a point.

JOAN. I never obeyed anyone. They all obeyed me.

NIJO. And what did you wear? He didn't make you get married in your own clothes? That would be perverse.*

MARLENE. Oh, you wait.

GRISELDA. *He had ladies with him who undressed me and they had a white silk dress and jewels for my hair.

MARLENE. And at first he seemed perfectly normal?

GRISELDA. Marlene, you're always so critical of him. / Of course he was normal, he was very kind.

MARLENE. But Griselda, come on, he took your baby.

GRISELDA. Walter found it hard to believe I loved him. He couldn't believe I would always obey him. He had to prove it.

MARLENE. I don't think Walter likes women.

GRISELDA. I'm sure he loved me, Marlene, all the time.

MARLENE. He just had a funny way / of showing it.

GRISELDA. It was hard for him too.

JOAN. How do you mean he took away your baby?

NIJO. Was it a boy?

GRISELDA. No, the first one was a girl.

NIJO. Even so it's hard when they take it away. Did you see it at all?

GRISELDA. Oh yes, she was six weeks old.

NIJO. Much better to do it straight away.

ISABELLA. But why did your husband take the child?

GRISELDA. He said all the people hated me because I was just one of them. And now I had a child they were restless. So he had to get rid of the child to keep them quiet. But he said he wouldn't snatch her, I had to agree and obey and give her up. So when I was feeding her a man came in and took her away. I thought he was going to kill her even before he was out of the room.

MARLENE. But you let him take her? You didn't struggle?

GRISELDA. I asked him to give her back so I could kiss her. And I asked him to bury her where no animals could dig her up. / It

ISABELLA. Oh my dear.

GRISELDA. was Walter's child to do what he liked with.*

MARLENE. Walter was bonkers.

GRET. Bastard.

ISABELLA. *But surely, murder.

GRISELDA. I had promised.

MARLENE. I can't stand this. I'm going for a pee.

MARLENE *goes out.*

The WAITRESS *brings dessert.*

NIJO. No, I understand. Of course you had to, he was your life. And were you in favour after that?

GRISELDA. Oh yes, we were very happy together. We never spoke about what had happened.

ISABELLA. I can see you were doing what you thought was your duty. But didn't it make you ill?

GRISELDA. No, I was very well, thank you.

NIJO. And you had another child?

GRISELDA. Not for four years, but then I did, yes, a boy.

NIJO. Ah a boy. / So it all ended happily.

GRISELDA. Yes he was pleased. I kept my son till he was two years old. A peasant's grandson. It made the people angry. Walter explained.

ISABELLA. But surely he wouldn't kill his children / just because —

GRISELDA. Oh it wasn't true. Walter would never give in to the people. He wanted to see if I loved him enough.

JOAN. He killed his children / to see if you loved him enough?

NIJO. Was it easier the second time or harder?

GRISELDA. It was always easy because I always knew I would do what he said.

Pause. They start to eat.

ISABELLA. I hope you didn't have any more children.

GRISELDA. Oh no, no more. It was twelve years till he tested me again.

ISABELLA. So whatever did he do this time ? / My poor John, I never loved him enough, and he would never have dreamt . . .

GRISELDA. He sent me away. He said the people wanted him to marry someone else who'd give him an heir and he'd got special permission from the Pope. So I said I'd go home to my father. I came with nothing / so I went with nothing. I

NIJO. Better to leave if your master doesn't want you.

GRISELDA. took off my clothes. He let me keep a slip so he wouldn't be shamed. And I walked home barefoot. My father came out in tears. Everyone was crying except me.

NIJO. At least your father wasn't dead. / I had nobody.

ISABELLA. Well it can be a relief to come home. I loved to see Hennie's sweet face again.

GRISELDA. Oh yes, I was perfectly content. And quite soon he sent for me again.

JOAN. I don't think I would have gone.

GRISELDA. But he told me to come. I had to obey him. He wanted me to help prepare his wedding. He was getting married to a young girl from France / and nobody except me knew how to arrange things the way he liked them.

NIJO. It's always hard taking him another woman.

MARLENE *comes back.*

JOAN. I didn't live a woman's life. I don't understand it.

GRISELDA. The girl was sixteen and far more beautiful than me. I could see why he loved her. / She had her younger brother with her as a page.

The WAITRESS *enters.*

MARLENE. Oh God, I can't bear it. I want some coffee. Six coffees. Six brandies. / Double brandies. Straightaway.

GRISELDA. They all went in to the feast I'd prepared. And he stayed behind and put his arms round me and kissed me. / I felt half asleep with the shock.

NIJO. Oh, like a dream.

MARLENE. And he said, 'This is your daughter and your son.'

GRISELDA. Yes.

JOAN. What?

NIJO. Oh. Oh I see. You got them back.

ISABELLA. I did think it was remarkably barbaric to kill them but you learn not to say anything. / So he had them brought up secretly I suppose.

MARLENE. Walter's a monster. Weren't you angry? What did you do?

GRISELDA. Well I fainted. Then I cried and kissed the children. / Everyone was making a fuss of me.

NIJO. But did you feel anything for them?

GRISELDA. What?

NIJO. Did you feel anything for the children?

GRISELDA. Of course, I loved them.

JOAN. So you forgave him and lived with him?

GRISELDA. He suffered so much all those years.

ISABELLA. Hennie had the same sweet nature.

NIJO. So they dressed you again?

GRISELDA. Cloth of gold.

JOAN. I can't forgive anything.

MARLENE. You really are exceptional, Griselda.

NIJO. Nobody gave me back my children.

NIJO *cries. The* WAITRESS *brings brandies.*

ISABELLA. I can never be like Hennie. I was always so busy in England, a kind of business I detested. The very presence of people exhausted my emotional reserves. I could not be like

Hennie however I tried. I tried and was as ill as could be. The doctor suggested a steel net to support my head, the weight of my own head was too much for my diseased spine. / It is dangerous to put oneself in depressing circumstances. Why should I do it?

JOAN. Don't cry.

NIJO. My father and the Emperor both died in the autumn. So much pain.

JOAN. Yes, but don't cry.

NIJO. They wouldn't let me into the palace when he was dying. I hid in the room with his coffin, then I couldn't find where I'd left my shoes, I ran after the funeral procession in bare feet, I couldn't keep up. When I got there it was over, a few wisps of smoke in the sky, that's all that was left of him. What I want to know is, if I'd still been at court, would I have been allowed to wear full mourning?

MARLENE. I'm sure you would.

NIJO. Why do you say that? You don't know anything about it. Would I have been allowed to wear full mourning?

ISABELLA. How can people live in this dim pale island and wear our hideous clothes? I cannot and will not live the life of a lady.

NIJO. I'll tell you something that made me angry. I was eighteen, at the Full Moon Ceremony. They make a special rice gruel and stir it with their sticks, and then they beat their women across the loins so they'll have sons and not daughters. So the Emperor beat us all / very hard as usual — that's not it,

MARLENE. What a sod.

NIJO. Marlene, that's normal, what made us angry, he told his attendants they could beat us too. Well they had a wonderful time. / So Lady Genki and I made a plan, and the ladies all hid

The WAITRESS *has entered with coffees.*

MARLENE. I'd like another brandy please. Better make it six.

NIJO. in his rooms, and Lady Mashimizu stood guard with a stick

at the door, and when His Majesty came in Genki seized him
and I beat him till he cried out and promised he would never
order anyone to hit us again. Afterwards there was a terrible
fuss. The nobles were horrified. 'We wouldn't even dream of
stepping on your Majesty's shadow.' And I had hit him with a
stick. Yes, I hit him with a stick.

JOAN. Suave, mari magno turbantibus aequora ventis,
e terra magnum alterius spectare laborem;
non quia vexari quemquamst iucunda voluptas,
sed quibus ipse malis careas quia cernere suave est.
Suave etiam belli certamina magna tueri
per campos instructa tua sine parte pericli.
Sed nil dulcius est, bene quam munita tenere
edita doctrina sapientum templa serena, /
despicere unde queas alios passimque videre
errare atque viam palantis quaerere vitae,

GRISELDA. I do think — I do wonder — it would have been nicer
if Walter hadn't had to.

ISABELLA. Why should I? Why should I?

MARLENE. Of course not.

NIJO. I hit him with a stick.

JOAN. certare ingenio, contendere nobilitate,
noctes atque dies niti praestante labore
ad summas emergere opes retumque potiri.
O miseras / hominum mentis, o pectora caeca!*

ISABELLA. Oh miseras!

NIJO. *Pectora caeca.

JOAN. qualibus in tenebris vitae quantisque periclis
degitur hoc aevi quodcumquest! / nonne videre
nil aliud sibi naturam latrare, nisi utqui
corpore seiunctus dolor absit, mente fruatur

JOAN *subsides*.

GRET. We come into hell through a big mouth. Hell's black and
red. / It's like the village where I come from. There's a river and

MARLENE (*to* JOAN). Shut up, pet.

ISABELLA. Listen, she's been to hell.

GRET. a bridge and houses. There's places on fire like when the
    soldiers come. There's a big devil sat on a roof with a big hole
    in his arse and he's scooping stuff out of it with a big ladle and
    it's falling down on us, and it's money, so a lot of the women
    stop and get some. But most of us is fighting the devils.
    There's lots of little devils, our size, and we get them down all
    right and give them a beating. There's lots of funny creatures
    round your feet, you don't like to look, like rats and lizards,
    and nasty things, a bum with a face, and fish with legs, and
    faces on things that don't have faces on. But they don't hurt,
    you just keep going. Well we'd had worse, you see, we'd had
    the Spanish. We'd all had family killed. My big son die on a
    wheel. Birds eat him. My baby, a soldier run her through with
    a sword. I'd had enough, I was mad, I hate the bastards. I
    come out my front door that morning and shout till my
    neighbours come out and I said, 'Come on, we're going where
    the evil come from and pay the bastards out.' And they all
    come out just as they was / from baking or washing in their

NIJO. All the ladies come.

GRET. aprons, and we push down the street and the ground
    opens up and we go through a big mouth into a street just like
    ours but in hell. I've got a sword in my hand from somewhere
    and I fill a basket with gold cups they drink out of down
    there. You just keep running on and fighting / you didn't stop
    for nothing. Oh we give them devils such a beating.

NIJO. Take that, take that.

JOAN. Something something something mortisque timores
    tum vacuum pectus — damn.
    Quod si ridicula —
    something something on and on and on and something
    splendorem purpureai.

ISABELLA. I thought I would have a last jaunt up the west river
    in China. Why not? But the doctors were so very grave. I just
    went to Morocco. The sea was so wild I had to be landed by

ship's crane in a coal bucket. / My horse was a terror to me a

GRET. Coal bucket, good.

JOAN. nos in luce timemus
something
terrorem.

ISABELLA. powerful black charger.

NIJO *is laughing and crying.*
JOAN *gets up and is sick in a corner.*
MARLENE *is drinking* ISABELLA'*s brandy.*

So off I went to visit the Berber sheikhs in full blue trousers
and great brass spurs. I was the only European woman ever
to have seen the Emperor of Morocco. I was seventy years old.
What lengths to go to for a last chance of joy. I knew my
return of vigour was only temporary, but how marvellous
while it lasted.

ACT TWO

Scene One

Employment Agency. MARLENE *and* JEANINE.

MARLENE. Right Jeanine, you are Jeanine aren't you? Let's
have a look. Os and As. / No As, all those Os you probably

JEANINE. Six Os.

MARLENE. could have got an A. / Speeds, not brilliant, not too
bad.

JEANINE. I wanted to go to work.

MARLENE. Well, Jeanine, what's your present job like?

JEANINE. I'm a secretary.

MARLENE. Secretary or typist?

JEANINE. I did start as a typist but the last six months I've been
a secretary.

MARLENE. To?

JEANINE. To three of them, really, they share me. There's

Mr Ashford, he's the office manager, and Mr Philby / is sales,
and —

MARLENE. Quite a small place?

JEANINE. A bit small.

MARLENE. Friendly?

JEANINE. Oh it's friendly enough.

MARLENE. Prospects?

JEANINE. I don't think so, that's the trouble. Miss Lewis is
secretary to the managing director and she's been there
forever, and Mrs Bradford/ is —

MARLENE. So you want a job with better prospects?

JEANINE. I want a change.

MARLENE. So you'll take anything comparable?

JEANINE. No, I do want prospects. I want more money.

MARLENE. You're getting — ?

JEANINE. Hundred.

MARLENE. It's not bad you know. You're what? Twenty?

JEANINE. I'm saving to get married.

MARLENE. Does that mean you don't want a long-term job, Jeanine?

JEANINE. I might do.

MARLENE. Because where do the prospects come in? No kids for a bit?

JEANINE. Oh no, not kids, not yet.

MARLENE. So you won't tell them you're getting married?

JEANINE. Had I better not?

MARLENE. It would probably help.

JEANINE. I'm not wearing a ring. We thought we wouldn't spend on a ring.

MARLENE. Saves taking it off.

JEANINE. I wouldn't take it off.

MARLENE. There's no need to mention it when you go for an interview. / Now Jeanine do you have a feel for any particular

JEANINE. But what if they ask?

MARLENE. kind of company?

JEANINE. I thought advertising.

MARLENE. People often do think advertising. I have got a few vacancies but I think they're looking for something glossier.

JEANINE. You mean how I dress? / I can dress different. I

MARLENE. I mean experience.

JEANINE. dress like this on purpose for where I am now.

MARLENE. I have a marketing department here of a knitwear manufacturer. / Marketing is near enough advertising. Secretary

JEANINE. Knitwear?

MARLENE. to the marketing manager, he's thirty-five, married, I've sent him a girl before and she was happy, left to have a baby, you won't want to mention marriage there. He's very fair I think, good at his job, you won't have to nurse him along. Hundred and ten, so that's better than you're doing now.

JEANINE. I don't know.

MARLENE. I've a fairly small concern here, father and two sons, you'd have more say potentially, secretarial and reception duties, only a hundred but the job's going to grow with the concern and then you'll be in at the top with new girls coming in underneath you.

JEANINE. What is it they do?

MARLENE. Lampshades. / This would be my first choice for you.

JEANINE. Just lampshades?

MARLENE. There's plenty of different kinds of lampshade. So we'll send you there, shall we, and the knitwear second choice. Are you free to go for an interview any day they call you?

JEANINE. I'd like to travel.

MARLENE. We don't have any foreign clients. You'd have to go elsewhere.

JEANINE. Yes I know. I don't really . . . I just mean . . .

MARLENE. Does your fiancé want to travel?

JEANINE. I'd like a job where I was here in London and with him and everything but now and then — I expect it's silly. Are there jobs like that?

MARLENE. There's personal assistant to a top executive in a multinational. If that's the idea you need to be planning ahead. Is that where you want to be in ten years?

JEANINE. I might not be alive in ten years.

MARLENE. Yes but you will be. You'll have children.

JEANINE. I can't think about ten years.

MARLENE. You haven't got the speeds anyway. So I'll send you to these two shall I? You haven't been to any other agency? Just so we don't get crossed wires. Now Jeanine I want you to get one of these jobs, all right? If I send you that means I'm putting myself on the line for you. Your presentation's OK, you look fine, just be confident and go in there convinced that this is the best job for you and you're the best person for the job. If you don't believe it they won't believe it.

JEANINE. Do you believe it?

MARLENE. I think you could make me believe it if you put your mind to it.

JEANINE. Yes, all right.

Scene Two

JOYCE's *back yard. The house with back door is upstage. Downstage a shelter made of junk, made by children. Two girls,* ANGIE *and* KIT, *are in it, squashed together.* ANGIE *is 16,* KIT *is 12. They cannot be seen from the house.* JOYCE *calls from the house.*

JOYCE. Angie. Angie are you out there?

Silence. They keep still and wait. When nothing else happens they relax.

ANGIE. Wish she was dead.

KIT. Wanna watch *The Exterminator?*

ANGIE. You're sitting on my leg.

KIT. There's nothing on telly. We can have an ice cream. Angie?

ANGIE. Shall I tell you something?

KIT. Do you wanna watch *The Exterminator?*

ANGIE. It's X, innit.

KIT. I can get into Xs.

ANGIE. Shall I tell you something?

KIT. We'll go to something else. We'll go to Ipswich. What's on the Odeon?

ANGIE. She won't let me, will she?

KIT. Don't tell her.

ANGIE. I've no money.

KIT. I'll pay.

ANGIE. She'll moan though, won't she?

KIT. I'll ask her for you if you like.

ANGIE. I've no money, I don't want you to pay.

KIT. I'll ask her.

ANGIE. She don't like you.

KIT. I still got three pounds birthday money. Did she say she
   don't like me? I'll go by myself then.

ANGIE. Your mum don't let you. I got to take you.

KIT. She won't know.

ANGIE. You'd be scared who'd sit next to you.

KIT. No I wouldn't.
   She does like me anyway.
   Tell me then.

ANGIE. Tell you what?

KIT. It's you she doesn't like.

ANGIE. Well I don't like her so tough shit.

JOYCE (off). Angie. Angie. Angie. I know you're out there. I'm
   not coming out after you. You come in here.

   Silence. Nothing happens.

ANGIE. Last night when I was in bed. I been thinking yesterday
   could I make things move. You know, make things move
   by thinking about them without touching them. Last night
   I was in bed and suddenly a picture fell down off the wall.

KIT. What picture?

ANGIE. My gran, that picture. Not the poster. The photograph
   in the frame.

KIT. Had you done something to make it fall down?

ANGIE. I must have done.

KIT. But were you thinking about it?

ANGIE. Not about it, but about something.

KIT. I don't think that's very good.

ANGIE. You know the kitten?

KIT. Which one?

ANGIE. There only is one. The dead one.

KIT. What about it?

ANGIE. I heard it last night.

KIT. Where?

ANGIE. Out here. In the dark. What if I left you here in the dark all night?

KIT. You couldn't. I'd go home.

ANGIE. You couldn't.

KIT. I'd / go home.

ANGIE. No you couldn't, not if I said.

KIT. I could.

ANGIE. Then you wouldn't see anything. You'd just be ignorant.

KIT. I can see in the daytime.

ANGIE. No you can't. You can't hear it in the daytime.

KIT. I don't want to hear it.

ANGIE. You're scared that's all.

KIT. I'm not scared of anything.

ANGIE. You're scared of blood.

KIT. It's not the same kitten anyway. You just heard an old cat, / you just heard some old cat.

ANGIE. You don't know what I heard. Or what I saw. You don't know nothing because you're a baby.

KIT. You're sitting on me.

ANGIE. Mind my hair / you silly cunt.

KIT. Stupid fucking cow, I hate you.

ANGIE. I don't care if you do.

KIT. You're horrible.

ANGIE. I'm going to kill my mother and you're going to watch.

KIT. I'm not playing.

ANGIE. You're scared of blood.

KIT *puts her hand under her dress, brings it out with blood on her finger.*

KIT. There, see, I got my own blood, so.

ANGIE *takes* KIT's *hand and licks her finger.*

ANGIE. Now I'm a cannibal. I might turn into a vampire now.

KIT. That picture wasn't nailed up right.

ANGIE. You'll have to do that when I get mine.

KIT. I don't have to.

ANGIE. You're scared.

KIT. I'll do it, I might do it. I don't have to just because you say. I'll be sick on you.

ANGIE. I don't care if you are sick on me, I don't mind sick. I don't mind blood. If I don't get away from here I'm going to die.

KIT. I'm going home.

ANGIE. You can't go through the house. She'll see you.

KIT. I won't tell her.

ANGIE. Oh great, fine.

KIT. I'll say I was by myself. I'll tell her you're at my house and I'm going there to get you.

ANGIE. She knows I'm here, stupid.

KIT. Then why can't I go through the house?

ANGIE. Because I said not.

KIT. My mum don't like you anyway.

ANGIE. I don't want her to like me. She's a slag.

KIT. She is not.

ANGIE. She does it with everyone.

KIT. She does not.

ANGIE. You don't even know what it is.

KIT. Yes I do.

ANGIE. Tell me then.

KIT. We get it all at school, cleverclogs. It's on television. You haven't done it.

ANGIE. How do you know?

KIT. Because I know you haven't.

ANGIE. You know wrong then because I have.

KIT. Who with?

ANGIE. I'm not telling you / who with.

KIT. You haven't anyway.

ANGIE. How do you know?

KIT. Who with?

ANGIE. I'm not telling you.

KIT. You said you told me everything.

ANGIE. I was lying wasn't I?

KIT. Who with? You can't tell me who with because / you never —

ANGIE. Sh.

> JOYCE *has come out of the house. She stops half way across the yard and listens. They listen.*

JOYCE. You there Angie? Kit? You there Kitty? Want a cup of tea? I've got some chocolate biscuits. Come on now I'll put the kettle on. Want a choccy biccy, Angie?

They all listen and wait.

Fucking rotten little cunt. You can stay there and die. I'll lock the back door.

They all wait.

JOYCE *goes back to the house.*

ANGIE *and* KIT *sit in silence for a while.*

KIT. When there's a war, where's the safest place?

ANGIE. Nowhere.

KIT. New Zealand is, my mum said. Your skin's burned right off. Shall we go to New Zealand?

ANGIE. I'm not staying here.

KIT. Shall we go to New Zealand?

ANGIE. You're not old enough.

KIT. You're not old enough.

ANGIE. I'm old enough to get married.

KIT. You don't want to get married.

ANGIE. No but I'm old enough.

KIT. I'd find out where they were going to drop it and stand right in the place.

ANGIE. You couldn't find out.

KIT. Better than walking round with your skin dragging on the ground. Eugh. / Would you like walking round with your skin dragging on the ground?

ANGIE. You couldn't find out, stupid, it's a secret.

KIT. Where are you going?

ANGIE. I'm not telling you.

KIT. Why?

ANGIE. It's a secret.

KIT. But you tell me all your secrets.

ANGIE. Not the true secrets.

KIT. Yes you do.

ANGIE. No I don't.

KIT. I want to go somewhere away from the war.

ANGIE. Just forget the war.

KIT. I can't.

ANGIE. You have to. It's so boring.

KIT. I'll remember it at night.

ANGIE. I'm going to do something else anyway.

KIT. What? Angie come on. Angie.

ANGIE. It's a true secret.

KIT. It can't be worse than the kitten. And killing your mother. And the war.

ANGIE. Well I'm not telling you so you can die for all I care.

KIT. My mother says there's something wrong with you playing with someone my age. She says why haven't you got friends your own age. People your own age know there's something funny about you. She says you're a bad influence. She says she's going to speak to your mother.

ANGIE *twists* KIT's *arm till she cries out.*

ANGIE. Say you're a liar.

KIT. She said it not me.

ANGIE. Say you eat shit.

KIT. You can't make me.

ANGIE *lets go.*

ANGIE. I don't care anyway. I'm leaving.

KIT. Go on then.

ANGIE. You'll all wake up one morning and find I've gone.

KIT. Good.

ANGIE. I'm not telling you when.

KIT' Go on then.

ANGIE. I'm sorry I hurt you.

KIT. I'm tired.

ANGIE. Do you like me?

KIT. I don't know.

ANGIE. You do like me.

KIT. I'm going home.

> KIT *gets up.*

ANGIE. No you're not.

KIT. I'm tired.

ANGIE. She'll see you.

KIT. She'll give me a chocolate biscuit.

ANGIE. Kitty.

KIT. Tell me where you're going.

ANGIE. Sit down.

> KIT *sits in the hut again.*

KIT. Go on then.

ANGIE. Swear?

KIT. Swear.

ANGIE. I'm going to London. To see my aunt.

KIT. And what?

ANGIE. That's it.

KIT. I see my aunt all the time.

ANGIE. I don't see my aunt.

KIT. What's so special?

ANGIE. It is special. She's special.

KIT. Why?

ANGIE. She is.

KIT. Why?

ANGIE. She is.

KIT. Why?

ANGIE. My mother hates her.

KIT. Why?

ANGIE. Because she does.

KIT. Perhaps she's not very nice.

ANGIE. She is nice.

KIT. How do you know?

ANGIE. Because I know her.

KIT. You said you never see her.

ANGIE. I saw her last year. You saw her.

KIT. Did I?

ANGIE. Never mind.

KIT. I remember her. That aunt. What's so special?

ANGIE. She gets people jobs.

KIT. What's so special?

ANGIE. I think I'm my aunt's child. I think my mother's really my aunt.

KIT. Why?

ANGIE. Because she goes to America, now shut up.

KIT. I've been to London.

ANGIE. Now give us a cuddle and shut up because I'm sick.

KIT. You're sitting on my arm.

Silence.

JOYCE *comes out and comes up to them quietly.*

JOYCE. Come on.

KIT. Oh hello.

JOYCE. Time you went home.

KIT. We want to go to the Odeon.

JOYCE. What time?

KIT. Don't know.

JOYCE. What's on?

KIT. Don't know.

JOYCE. Don't know much do you?

KIT. That all right then?

JOYCE. Angie's got to clean her room first.

ANGIE. No I don't.

JOYCE. Yes you do, it's a pigsty.

ANGIE. Well I'm not.

JOYCE. Then you're not going. I don't care.

ANGIE. Well I am going.

JOYCE. You've no money, have you?

ANGIE. Kit's paying anyway.

JOYCE. No she's not.

KIT. I'll help you with your room.

JOYCE. That's nice.

ANGIE. No you won't. You wait here.

KIT. Hurry then.

ANGIE. I'm not hurrying. You just wait.

ANGIE *goes into the house. Silence.*

JOYCE. I don't know.

Silence.

How's school then?

KIT. All right.

JOYCE. What are you now? Third year?

KIT. Second year.

JOYCE. Your mum says you're good at English.

Silence.

Maybe Angie should've stayed on.

KIT. She didn't like it.

JOYCE. I didn't like it. And look at me. If your face fits at school it's going to fit other places too. It wouldn't make no difference to Angie. She's not going to get a job when jobs are hard to get. I'd be sorry for anyone in charge of her. She'd better get married. I don't know who'd have her, mind. She's one of those girls might never leave home. What do you want to be when you grow up, Kit?

KIT. Physicist.

JOYCE. What?

KIT. Nuclear physicist.

JOYCE. Whatever for?

KIT. I could, I'm clever.

JOYCE. I know you're clever, pet.

Silence.

I'll make a cup of tea.

Silence.

Looks like it's going to rain.

Silence.

Don't you have friends your own age?

KIT. Yes.

JOYCE. Well then.

KIT. I'm old for my age.

JOYCE. And Angie's simple is she? She's not simple.

KIT. I love Angie.

JOYCE. She's clever in her own way.

KIT. You can't stop me.

JOYCE. I don't want to.

KIT. You can't, so.

JOYCE. Don't be cheeky, Kitty. She's always kind to little children.

KIT. She's coming so you better leave me alone.

ANGIE *comes out. She has changed into an old best dress, slightly small for her.*

JOYCE. What you put that on for? Have you done your room? You can't clean your room in that.

ANGIE. I looked in the cupboard and it was there.

JOYCE. Of course it was there, it's meant to be there. Is that why it was a surprise, finding something in the right place? I should think she's surprised, wouldn't you Kit, to find something in her room in the right place.

ANGIE. I decided to wear it.

JOYCE. Not today, why? To clean your room? You're not going to the pictures till you've done your room. You can put your dress on after if you like.

ANGIE *picks up a brick.*

Have you done your room? You're not getting out of it, you know.

KIT. Angie, let's go.

JOYCE. She's not going till she's done her room.

KIT. It's starting to rain.

JOYCE. Come on, come on then. Hurry and do your room, Angie, and then you can go to the cinema with Kit. Oh it's wet, come on. We'll look up the time in the paper. Does your mother know, Kit, it's going to be a late night for you, isn't it? Hurry up, Angie. You'll spoil your dress. You make me sick.

JOYCE *and* KIT *run in.*

ANGIE *stays where she is. Sound of rain.*

KIT *comes out of the house and shouts.*

KIT. Angie. Angie, come on, you'll get wet.

KIT *comes back to* ANGIE.

ANGIE. I put on this dress to kill my mother.

KIT. I suppose you thought you'd do it with a brick.

ANGIE. You can kill people with a brick.

KIT. Well you didn't, so.

Scene Three

Office of 'Top Girls' Employment Agency. Three desks and a small interviewing area. Monday morning. WIN and NELL have just arrived for work.

NELL. Coffee coffee coffee coffee / coffee.

WIN. The roses were smashing. / Mermaid.

NELL. Ohhh.

WIN. Iceberg. He taught me all their names.

NELL *has some coffee now.*

NELL. Ah. Now then.

WIN. He has one of the finest rose gardens in West Sussex. He exhibits.

NELL. He what?

WIN. His wife was visiting her mother. It was like living together.

NELL. Crafty, you never said.

WIN. He rang on Saturday morning.

NELL. Lucky you were free.

WIN. That's what I told him.

NELL. Did you hell.

WIN. Have you ever seen a really beautiful rose garden?

NELL. I don't like flowers. / I like swimming pools.

WIN. Marilyn. Esther's Baby. They're all called after birds.

NELL. Our friend's late. Celebrating all weekend I bet you.

WIN. I'd call a rose Elvis. Or John Conteh.

NELL. Is Howard in yet?

WIN. If he is he'll be bleeping us with a problem.

NELL. Howard can just hang onto himself.

WIN. Howard's really cut up.

NELL. Howard thinks because he's a fella the job was his as of right. Our Marlene's got far more balls than Howard and that's that.

WIN. Poor little bugger.

NELL. He'll live.

WIN. He'll move on.

NELL. I wouldn't mind a change of air myself.

WIN. Serious?

NELL. I've never been a staying put lady. Pastures new.

WIN. So who's the pirate?

NELL. There's nothing definite.

WIN. Inquiries?

NELL. There's always inquiries. I'd think I'd got bad breath if there stopped being inquiries. Most of them can't afford me. Or you.

WIN. I'm all right for the time being. Unless I go to Australia.

NELL. There's not a lot of room upward.

WIN. Marlene's filled it up.

NELL. Good luck to her. Unless there's some prospects moneywise.

WIN. You can but ask.

NELL. Can always but ask.

WIN. So what have we got? I've got a Mr Holden I saw last week.

NELL. Any use?

WIN. Pushy. Bit of a cowboy.

NELL. Good-looker?

WIN. Good dresser.

NELL. High flyer?

WIN. That's his general idea certainly but I'm not sure he's got it up there.

NELL. Prestel wants six high flyers and I've only seen two and a half.

WIN. He's making a bomb on the road but he thinks it's time for an office. I sent him to IBM but he didn't get it.

NELL. Prestel's on the road.

WIN. He's not overbright.

NELL. Can he handle an office?

WIN. Provided his secretary can punctuate he should go far.

NELL. Bear Prestel in mind then, I might put my head round the door. I've got that poor little nerd I should never have said I could help. Tender heart me.

WIN. Tender like old boots. How old?

NELL. Yes well forty-five.

WIN. Say no more.

NELL. He knows his place, he's not after calling himself a manager, he's just a poor little bod wants a better commission and a bit of sunshine.

WIN. Don't we all.

NELL. He's just got to relocate. He's got a bungalow in Dymchurch.

WIN. And his wife says.

NELL. The lady wife wouldn't care to relocate. She's going through the change.

WIN. It's his funeral, don't waste your time.

NELL. I don't waste a lot.

WIN. Good weekend you?

NELL. You could say.

WIN. Which one?

NELL. One Friday, one Saturday.

WIN. Aye aye.

NELL. Sunday night I watched telly.

WIN. Which of them do you like best really?

NELL. Sunday was best, I liked the Ovaltine.

WIN. Holden, Barker, Gardner, Duke.

NELL. I've a lady here thinks she can sell.

WIN. Taking her on?

NELL. She's had some jobs.

WIN. Services?

NELL. No, quite heavy stuff, electric.

WIN. Tough bird like us.

NELL. We could do with a few more here.

WIN. There's nothing going here.

NELL. No but I always want the tough ones when I see them. Hang onto them.

WIN. I think we're plenty.

NELL. Derek asked me to marry him again.

WIN. He doesn't know when he's beaten.

NELL. I told him I'm not going to play house, not even in Ascot.

WIN. Mind you, you could play house.

NELL. If I chose to play house I would play house ace.

WIN. You could marry him and go on working.

NELL. I could go on working and not marry him.

   MARLENE *arrives*.

MARLENE. Morning ladies.

WIN *and* NELL *cheer and whistle.*

Mind my head.

NELL. Coffee coffee coffee.

WIN. We're tactfully not mentioning you're late.

MARLENE. Fucking tube.

WIN. We've heard that one.

NELL. We've used that one.

WIN. It's the top executive doesn't come in as early as the poor working girl.

MARLENE. Pass the sugar and shut your face, pet.

WIN. Well I'm delighted.

NELL. Howard's looking sick.

WIN. Howard is sick. He's got ulcers and heart. He told me.

NELL. He'll have to stop then won't he?

WIN. Stop what?

NELL. Smoking, drinking, shouting. Working.

WIN. Well, working.

NELL. We're just looking through the day.

MARLENE. I'm doing some of Pam's ladies. They've been piling up while she's away.

NELL. Half a dozen little girls and an arts graduate who can't type.

WIN. I spent the whole weekend at his place in Sussex.

NELL. She fancies his rose garden.

WIN. I had to lie down in the back of the car so the neighbours wouldn't see me go in.

NELL. You're kidding.

WIN. It was funny.

NELL. Fuck that for a joke.

WIN. It was funny.

MARLENE. Anyway they'd see you in the garden.

WIN. The garden has extremely high walls.

NELL. I think I'll tell the wife.

WIN. Like hell.

NELL. She might leave him and you could have the rose garden.

WIN. The minute it's not a secret I'm out on my ear.

NELL. Don't know why you bother.

WIN. Bit of fun.

NELL. I think it's time you went to Australia.

WIN. I think it's pushy Mr Holden time.

NELL. If you've any really pretty bastards, Marlene, I want some for Prestel.

MARLENE. I might have one this afternoon. This morning it's all Pam's secretarial.

NELL. Not long now and you'll be upstairs watching over us all.

MARLENE. Do you feel bad about it?

NELL. I don't like coming second.

MARLENE. Who does?

WIN. We'd rather it was you than Howard. We're glad for you, aren't we Nell.

NELL. Oh yes. Aces.

Interview
WIN *and* LOUISE.

WIN. Now Louise, hello, I have your details here. You've been very loyal to the one job I see.

LOUISE. Yes I have.

WIN. Twenty-one years is a long time in one place.

LOUISE. I feel it is. I feel it's time to move on.

WIN. And you are what age now?

LOUISE. I'm in my early forties.

WIN. Exactly?

LOUISE. Forty-six.

WIN. It's not necessarily a handicap, well it is of course we have to face that, but it's not necessarily a disabling handicap, experience does count for something.

LOUISE. I hope so.

WIN. Now between ourselves is there any trouble, any reason why you're leaving that wouldn't appear on the form?

LOUISE. Nothing like that.

WIN. Like what?

LOUISE. Nothing at all.

WIN. No long term understandings come to a sudden end, making for an insupportable atmosphere?

LOUISE. I've always completely avoided anything like that at all.

WIN. No personality clashes with your immediate superiors or inferiors?

LOUISE. I've always taken care to get on very well with everyone.

WIN. I only ask because it can affect the reference and it also affects your motivation, I want to be quite clear why you're moving on. So I take it the job itself no longer satisfies you. Is it the money?

LOUISE. It's partly the money. It's not so much the money.

WIN. Nine thousand is very respectable. Have you dependants?

LOUISE. No, no dependants. My mother died.

WIN. So why are you making a change?

LOUISE. Other people make changes.

WIN. But why are you, now, after spending most of your life in the one place?

LOUISE. There you are, I've lived for that company, I've given my life really you could say because I haven't had a great deal of social life, I've worked in the evenings. I haven't had office entanglements for the very reason you just mentioned and if you are committed to your work you don't move in many other circles. I had management status from the age of twenty-seven and you'll appreciate what that means. I've built up a department. And there it is, it works extremely well, and I feel I'm stuck there. I've spent twenty years in middle management. I've seen young men who I trained go on, in my own company or elsewhere, to higher things. Nobody notices me, I don't expect it, I don't attract attention by making mistakes, everybody takes it for granted that my work is perfect. They will notice me when I go, they will be sorry I think to lose me, they will offer me more money of course, I will refuse. They will see when I've gone what I was doing for them.

WIN. If they offer you more money you won't stay?

LOUISE. No I won't.

WIN. Are you the only woman?

LOUISE. Apart from the girls of course, yes. There was one, she was my assistant, it was the only time I took on a young woman assistant, I always had my doubts. I don't care greatly for working with women, I think I pass as a man at work. But I did take on this young woman, her qualifications were excellent, and she did well, she got a department of her own, and left the company for a competitor where she's now on the board and good luck to her. She has a different style, she's a new kind of attractive well-dressed — I don't mean I don't dress properly. But there is a kind of woman who is thirty now who grew up in a different climate. They are not so careful. They take themselves for granted. I have had to justify my existence every minute, and I have done so, I have proved — well.

WIN. Let's face it, vacancies are going to be ones where you'll be in competition with younger men. And there are companies that will value your experience enough you'll be in with a chance. There are also fields that are easier for a woman, there is a cosmetic company here where your experience might be relevant. It's eight and a half, I don't know if that appeals.

LOUISE. I've proved I can earn money. It's more important to get away. I feel it's now or never. I sometimes / think —

WIN. You shouldn't talk too much at an interview.

LOUISE. I don't. I don't normally talk about myself. I know very well how to handle myself in an office situation. I only talk to you because it seems to me this is different, it's your job to understand me, surely. You asked the questions.

WIN. I think I understand you sufficiently.

LOUISE. Well good, that's good.

WIN. Do you drink?

LOUISE. Certainly not. I'm not a teetotaller, I think that's very suspect, it's seen as being an alcoholic if you're teetotal. What do you mean? I don't drink. Why?

WIN. I drink.

LOUISE. I don't.

WIN. Good for you.

Main office
MARLENE *and* ANGIE.
ANGIE *arrives.*

ANGIE. Hello.

MARLENE. Have you an appointment?

ANGIE. It's me. I've come.

MARLENE. What? It's not Angie?

ANGIE. It was hard to find this place. I got lost.

MARLENE. How did you get past the receptionist? The girl on the desk, didn't she try to stop you?

ANGIE. What desk?

MARLENE. Never mind.

ANGIE. I just walked in. I was looking for you.

MARLENE. Well you found me.

ANGIE. Yes.

MARLENE. So where's your mum? Are you up in town for the day?

ANGIE. Not really.

MARLENE. Sit down. Do you feel all right?

ANGIE. Yes thank you.

MARLENE. So where's Joyce?

ANGIE. She's at home.

MARLENE. Did you come up on a school trip then?

ANGIE. I've left school.

MARLENE. Did you come up with a friend?

ANGIE. No. There's just me.

MARLENE. You came up by yourself, that's fun. What have you been doing? Shopping? Tower of London?

ANGIE. No, I just come here. I come to you.

MARLENE. That's very nice of you to think of paying your aunty a visit. There's not many nieces make that the first port of call. Would you like a cup of coffee?

ANGIE. No thank you.

MARLENE. Tea, orange?

ANGIE. No thank you.

MARLENE. Do you feel all right?

ANGIE. Yes thank you.

MARLENE. Are you tired from the journey?

ANGIE. Yes, I'm tired from the journey.

MARLENE. You sit there for a bit then. How's Joyce?

ANGIE. She's all right.

MARLENE. Same as ever.

ANGIE. Oh yes.

MARLENE. Unfortunately you've picked a day when I'm rather busy, if there's ever a day when I'm not, or I'd take you out to lunch and we'd go to Madame Tussaud's. We could go shopping. What time do you have to be back? Have you got a day return?

ANGIE. No.

MARLENE. So what train are you going back on?

ANGIE. I came on the bus.

MARLENE. So what bus are you going back on? Are you staying the night?

ANGIE. Yes.

MARLENE. Who are you staying with? Do you want me to put you up for the night, is that it?

ANGIE. Yes please.

MARLENE. I haven't got a spare bed.

ANGIE. I can sleep on the floor.

MARLENE. You can sleep on the sofa.

ANGIE. Yes please.

MARLENE. I do think Joyce might have phoned me. It's like her.

ANGIE. This is where you work is it?

MARLENE. It's where I have been working the last two years but I'm going to move into another office.

ANGIE. It's lovely.

MARLENE. My new office is nicer than this. There's just the one big desk in it for me.

ANGIE. Can I see it?

MARLENE. Not now, no, there's someone else in it now. But he's leaving at the end of next week and I'm going to do his job.

ANGIE. Is that good?

MARLENE. Yes, it's very good.

ANGIE. Are you going to be in charge?

MARLENE. Yes I am.

ANGIE. I knew you would be.

MARLENE. How did you know?

ANGIE. I knew you'd be in charge of everything.

MARLENE. Not quite everything.

ANGIE. You will be.

MARLENE. Well we'll see.

ANGIE. Can I see it next week then?

MARLENE. Will you still be here next week?

ANGIE. Yes.

MARLENE. Don't you have to go home?

ANGIE. No.

MARLENE. Why not?

ANGIE. It's all right.

MARLENE. Is it all right?

ANGIE. Yes, don't worry about it.

MARLENE. Does Joyce know where you are?

ANGIE. Yes of course she does.

MARLENE..Well does she?

ANGIE. Don't worry about it.

MARLENE. How long are you planning to stay with me then?

ANGIE. You know when you came to see us last year?

MARLENE. Yes, that was nice wasn't it?

ANGIE. That was the best day of my whole life.

MARLENE. So how long are you planning to stay?

ANGIE. Don't you want me?

MARLENE. Yes yes, I just wondered.

ANGIE. I won't stay if you don't want me.

MARLENE. No, of course you can stay.

ANGIE. I'll sleep on the floor. I won't be any bother.

MARLENE. Don't get upset.

ANGIE. I'm not, I'm not. Don't worry about it.

MRS KIDD *comes in.*

MRS KIDD. Excuse me.

MARLENE. Yes.

MRS KIDD. Excuse me.

MARLENE. Can I help you?

MRS KIDD. Excuse me bursting in on you like this but I have to talk to you.

MARLENE. I am engaged at the moment. / If you could go to reception —

MRS KIDD. I'm Rosemary Kidd, Howard's wife, you don't recognise me but we did meet, I remember you of course / but you wouldn't —

MARLENE. Yes of course, Mrs Kidd, I'm sorry, we did meet. Howard's about somewhere I expect, have you looked in his office?

MRS KIDD. Howard's not about, no. I'm afraid it's you I've come to see if I could have a minute or two.

MARLENE. I do have an appointment in five minutes.

MRS KIDD. This won't take five minutes. I'm very sorry. It is a matter of some urgency.

MARLENE. Well of course. What can I do for you?

MRS KIDD. I just wanted a chat, an informal chat. It's not something I can simply — I'm sorry if I'm interrupting your work. I know office work isn't like housework / which is all interruptions.

MARLENE. No no, this is my niece. Angie. Mrs Kidd.

MRS KIDD. Very pleased to meet you.

ANGIE. Very well thank you.

MRS KIDD. Howard's not in today.

MARLENE. Isn't he?

MRS KIDD. He's feeling poorly.

MARLENE. I didn't know. I'm sorry to hear that.

MRS KIDD. The fact is he's in a state of shock. About what's happened.

MARLENE. What has happened?

MRS KIDD. You should know if anyone. I'm referring to you being appointed managing director instead of Howard. He hasn't been at all well all weekend. He hasn't slept for three nights. I haven't slept.

MARLENE. I'm sorry to hear that, Mrs Kidd. Has he thought of taking sleeping pills?

MRS KIDD. It's very hard when someone has worked all these years.

MARLENE. Business life is full of little setbacks. I'm sure Howard knows that. He'll bounce back in a day or two. We all bounce back.

MRS KIDD. If you could see him you'd know what I'm talking about. What's it going to do to him working for a woman? I think if it was a man he'd get over it as something normal.

MARLENE. I think he's going to have to get over it.

MRS KIDD. It's me that bears the brunt. I'm not the one that's been promoted. I put him first every inch of the way. And now what do I get? You women this, you women that. It's not my fault. You're going to have to be very careful how you handle him. He's very hurt.

MARLENE. Naturally I'll be tactful and pleasant to him, you don't start pushing someone round. I'll consult him over any decisions affecting his department. But that's no different, Mrs Kidd, from any of my other colleagues.

MRS KIDD. I think it is different, because he's a man.

MARLENE. I'm not quite sure why you came to see me.

MRS KIDD. I had to do something.

MARLENE. Well you've done it, you've seen me. I think that's probably all we've time for. I'm sorry he's been taking it out on you. He really is a shit, Howard.

MRS KIDD. But he's got a family to support. He's got three children. It's only fair.

MARLENE. Are you suggesting I give up the job to him then?

MRS KIDD. It had crossed my mind if you were unavailable after all for some reason, he would be the natural second choice I think, don't you? I'm not asking.

MARLENE. Good.

MRS KIDD. You mustn't tell him I came. He's very proud.

MARLENE. If he doesn't like what's happening here he can go and work somewhere else.

MRS KIDD. Is that a threat?

MARLENE. I'm sorry but I do have some work to do.

MRS KIDD. It's not that easy, a man of Howard's age. You don't care. I thought he was going too far but he's right. You're one of these ballbreakers / that's what you are. You'll end up

MARLENE. I'm sorry but I do have some work to do.

MRS KIDD. miserable and lonely. You're not natural.

MARLENE. Could you please piss off?

MRS KIDD. I thought if I saw you at least I'd be doing something.

MRS KIDD *goes.*

MARLENE. I've got to go and do some work now. Will you come back later?

ANGIE. I think you were wonderful.

MARLENE. I've got to go and do some work now.

ANGIE. You told her to piss off.

MARLENE. Will you come back later?

ANGIE. Can't I stay here?

MARLENE. Don't you want to go sightseeing?

ANGIE. I'd rather stay here.

MARLENE. You can stay here I suppose, if it's not boring.

ANGIE. It's where I most want to be in the world.

MARLENE. I'll see you later then.

> MARLENE *goes.*

> ANGIE *sits at* WIN's *desk.*

Interview

NELL *and* SHONA.

NELL. Is this right? You are Shona?

SHONA. Yeh.

NELL. It says here you're twenty-nine.

SHONA. Yeh.

NELL. Too many late nights, me. So you've been where you are for four years, Shona, you're earning six basic and three commission. So what's the problem?

SHONA. No problem.

NELL. Why do you want a change?

SHONA. Just a change.

NELL. Change of product, change of area?

SHONA. Both.

NELL. But you're happy on the road?

SHONA. I like driving.

NELL. You're not after management status?

SHONA. I would like management status.

NELL. You'd be interested in titular management status but not come off the road?

SHONA. I want to be on the road, yeh.

NELL. So how many calls have you been making a day?

SHONA. Six.

NELL. And what proportion of those are successful?

SHONA. Six.

NELL. That's hard to believe.

SHONA. Four.

NELL. You find it easy to get the initial interest do you?

SHONA. Oh yeh, I get plenty of initial interest.

NELL. And what about closing?

SHONA. I close, don't I?

NELL. Because that's what an employer is going to have doubts
    about with a lady as I needn't tell you, whether she's got
    the guts to push through to a closing situation. They think
    we're too nice. They think we listen to the buyer's doubts.
    They think we consider his needs and his feelings.

SHONA. I never consider people's feelings.

NELL. I was selling for six years, I can sell anything, I've sold in
    three continents, and I'm jolly as they come but I'm not
    very nice.

SHONA. I'm not very nice.

NELL. What sort of time do you have on the road with the other
    reps? Get on all right? Handle the chat?

SHONA. I get on. Keep myself to myself.

NELL. Fairly much of a loner are you?

SHONA. Sometimes.

NELL. So what field are you interested in?

SHONA. Computers.

NELL. That's a top field as you know and you'll be up against
    some very slick fellas there, there's some very pretty boys in
    computers, it's an American-style field.

SHONA. That's why I want to do it.

NELL. Video systems appeal? That's a high-flying situation.

SHONA. Video systems appeal OK.

NELL. Because Prestel have half a dozen vacancies I'm looking to fill at the moment. We're talking in the area of ten to fifteen thousand here and upwards.

SHONA. Sounds OK.

NELL. I've half a mind to go for it myself. But it's good money here if you've got the top clients. Could you fancy it do you think?

SHONA. Work here?

NELL. I'm not in a position to offer, there's nothing officially going just now, but we're always on the lookout. There's not that many of us. We could keep in touch.

SHONA. I like driving.

NELL. So the Prestel appeals?

SHONA. Yeh.

NELL. What about ties?

SHONA. No ties.

NELL. So relocation wouldn't be a problem.

SHONA. No problem.

NELL. So just fill me in a bit more could you about what you've been doing.

SHONA. What I've been doing. It's all down there.

NELL. The bare facts are down here but I've got to present you to an employer.

SHONA. I'm twenty-nine years old.

NELL. So it says here.

SHONA. We look young. Youngness runs in the family in our family.

NELL. So just describe your present job for me.

SHONA. My present job at present. I have a car. I have a Porsche.
I go up the M1 a lot. Burn up the M1 a lot. Straight up the
M1 in the fast lane to where the clients are, Staffordshire,
Yorkshire, I do a lot in Yorkshire. I'm selling electric things.
Like dishwashers, washing machines, stainless steel tubs are
a feature and the reliability of the programme. After sales
service, we offer a very good after sales service, spare parts,
plenty of spare parts. And fridges, I sell a lot of fridges
specially in the summer. People want to buy fridges in the
summer because of the heat melting the butter and you get fed
up standing the milk in a basin of cold water with a cloth
over, stands to reason people don't want to do that in this
day and age. So I sell a lot of them. Big ones with big freezers.
Big freezers. And I stay in hotels at night when I'm away from
home. On my expense account. I stay in various hotels. They
know me, the ones I go to. I check in, have a bath, have a
shower. Then I go down to the bar, have a gin and tonic, have
a chat. Then I go into the dining room and have dinner. I
usually have fillet steak and mushrooms, I like mushrooms.
I like smoked salmon very much. I like having a salad on the
side. Green salad. I don't like tomatoes.

NELL. Christ what a waste of time.

SHONA. Beg your pardon?

NELL. Not a word of this is true is it?

SHONA. How do you mean?

NELL. You just filled in the form with a pack of lies.

SHONA. Not exactly.

NELL. How old are you?

SHONA. Twenty-nine.

NELL. Nineteen?

SHONA. Twenty-one.

NELL. And what jobs have you done? Have you done any?

SHONA. I could though, I bet you.

Main office
ANGIE *sitting as before.*
WIN *comes in.*

WIN. Who's sitting in my chair?

ANGIE. What? Sorry.

WIN. Who's been eating my porridge?

ANGIE. What?

WIN. It's all right, I saw Marlene. Angie isn't it? I'm Win. And I'm not going out for lunch because I'm knackered. I'm going to set me down here and have a yoghurt. Do you like yoghurt?

ANGIE. No.

WIN. That's good because I've only got one. Are you hungry?

ANGIE. No.

WIN. There's a cafe on the corner.

ANGIE. No thank you. Do you work here?

WIN. How did you guess?

ANGIE. Because you look as if you might work here and you're sitting at the desk. Have you always worked here?

WIN. No I was headhunted. That means I was working for another outfit like this and this lot came and offered me more money. I broke my contract, there was a hell of a stink. There's not many top ladies about. Your aunty's a smashing bird.

ANGIE. Yes I know.

MARLENE. Fan are you? Fan of your aunty's?

ANGIE. Do you think I could work here?

WIN. Not at the moment.

ANGIE. How do I start?

WIN. What can you do?

ANGIE. I don't know. Nothing.

WIN. Type?

ANGIE. Not very well. The letters jump up when I do capitals. I was going to do a CSE in commerce but I didn't.

WIN. What have you got?

ANGIE. What?

WIN. CSE's, O's.

ANGIE. Nothing, none of that. Did you do all that?

WIN. Oh yes, all that, and a science degree funnily enough. I started out doing medical research but there's no money in it. I thought I'd go abroad. Did you know they sell Coca-Cola in Russia and Pepsi-cola in China? You don't have to be qualified as much as you might think. Men are awful bullshitters, they like to make out jobs are harder than they are. Any job I ever did I started doing it better than the rest of the crowd and they didn't like it. So I'd get unpopular and I'd have a drink to cheer myself up. I lived with a fella and supported him for four years, he couldn't get work. After that I went to California. I like the sunshine. Americans know how to live. This country's too slow. Then I went to Mexico, still in sales, but it's no country for a single lady. I came home, went bonkers for a bit, thought I was five different people, got over that all right, the psychiatrist said I was perfectly sane and highly intelligent. Got married in a moment of weakness and he's inside now, he's been inside four years, and I've not been to see him too much this last year. I like this better than sales, I'm not really that aggressive. I started thinking sales was a good job if you want to meet people, but you're meeting people that don't want to meet you. It's no good if you like being liked. Here your clients want to meet you because you're the one doing them some good. They hope.

ANGIE *has fallen asleep.* NELL *comes in.*

NELL. You're talking to yourself, sunshine.

WIN. So what's new?

NELL. Who is this?

WIN. Marlene's little niece.

NELL. What's she got, brother, sister? She never talks about her family.

WIN. I was telling her my life story.

NELL. Violins?

WIN. No, success story.

NELL. You've heard Howard's had a heart attack?

WIN. No, when?

NELL. I heard just now. He hadn't come in, he was at home, he's gone to hospital. He's not dead. His wife was here, she rushed off in a cab.

WIN. Too much butter, too much smoke. We must send him some flowers.

MARLENE *comes in.*

You've heard about Howard?

MARLENE. Poor sod.

NELL. Lucky he didn't get the job if that's what his health's like.

MARLENE. Is she asleep?

WIN. She wants to work here.

MARLENE. Packer in Tesco more like.

WIN. She's a nice kid. Isn't she?

MARLENE. She's a bit thick. She's a bit funny.

WIN. She thinks you're wonderful.

MARLENE. She's not going to make it.

ACT THREE

A year earlier. Sunday evening. JOYCE's *kitchen.* JOYCE,
ANGIE, MARLENE. MARLENE *is taking presents out of a*
bright carrier bag. ANGIE *has already opened a box of*
chocolates.

MARLENE. Just a few little things. / I've no memory for

JOYCE. There's no need.

MARLENE. birthdays have I, and Christmas seems to slip by. So
I think I owe Angie a few presents.

JOYCE. What do you say?

ANGIE. Thank you very much. Thank you very much, Aunty
Marlene.

She opens a present. It is the dress from Act One, new.

ANGIE. Oh look, Mum, isn't it lovely?

MARLENE. I don't know if it's the right size. She's grown up
since I saw her. / I knew she was always tall for her age.

ANGIE. Isn't it lovely?

JOYCE. She's a big lump.

MARLENE. Hold it up, Angie, let's see.

ANGIE. I'll put it on, shall I?

MARLENE. Yes, try it on.

JOYCE. Go on to your room then, we don't want / a strip show
thank you.

ANGIE. Of course I'm going to my room, what do you think?
Look Mum, here's something for you. Open it, go on. What
is it? Can I open it for you?

JOYCE. Yes, you open it, pet.

ANGIE. Don't you want to open it yourself? / Go on.

JOYCE. I don't mind, you can do it.

ANGIE. It's something hard. It's — what is it? A bottle. Drink is it? No, it's what? Perfume, look. What a lot. Open it, look, let's smell it. Oh it's strong. It's lovely. Put it on me. How do you do it? Put it on me.

JOYCE. You're too young.

ANGIE. I can play wearing it like dressing up.

JOYCE. And you're too old for that. Here, give it here, I'll do it, you'll tip the whole bottle over yourself / and we'll have you smelling all summer.

ANGIE. Put it on you. Do I smell? Put it on Aunty too. Put it on Aunty too. Let's all smell.

MARLENE. I didn't know what you'd like.

JOYCE. There's no danger I'd have it already, / that's one thing.

ANGIE. Now we all smell the same.

MARLENE. It's a bit of nonsense.

JOYCE. It's very kind of you Marlene, you shouldn't.

ANGIE. Now. I'll put on the dress and then we'll see.

ANGIE *goes.*

JOYCE. You've caught me on the hop with the place in a mess. / If you'd let me know you was coming I'd have got

MARLENE. That doesn't matter.

JOYCE. something in to eat. We had our dinner dinnertime. We're just going to have a cup of tea. You could have an egg.

MARLENE. No, I'm not hungry. Tea's fine.

JOYCE. I don't expect you take sugar.

MARLENE. Why not?

JOYCE. You take care of yourself.

MARLENE. How do you mean you didn't know I was coming?

JOYCE. You could have written. I know we're not on the phone but we're not completely in the dark ages, / we do have a postman.

MARLENE. But you asked me to come.

JOYCE. How did I ask you to come?

MARLENE. Angie said when she phoned up.

JOYCE. Angie phoned up, did she?

MARLENE. Was it just Angie's idea?

JOYCE. What did she say?

MARLENE. She said you wanted me to come and see you. /
     It was a couple of weeks ago. How was I to know that's a

JOYCE. Ha.

MARLENE. ridiculous idea? My diary's always full a couple of
     weeks ahead so we fixed it for this weekend. I was meant to
     get here earlier but I was held up. She gave me messages from
     you.

JOYCE. Didn't you wonder why I didn't phone you myself?

MARLENE. She said you didn't like using the phone. You're shy
     on the phone and can't use it. I don't know what you're like,
     do I.

JOYCE. Are there people who can't use the phone?

MARLENE. I expect so.

JOYCE. I haven't met any.

MARLENE. Why should I think she was lying?

JOYCE. Because she's like what she's like.

MARLENE. How do I know / what she's like?

JOYCE. It's not my fault you don't know what she's like. You
     never come and see her.

MARLENE. Well I have now / and you don't seem over the moon.*

JOYCE. Good.
     *Well I'd have got a cake if she'd told me.

     Pause.

MARLENE. I did wonder why you wanted to see me.

JOYCE. I didn't want to see you.

MARLENE. Yes, I know. Shall I go?

JOYCE. I don't mind seeing you.

MARLENE. Great, I feel really welcome.

JOYCE. You can come and see Angie any time you like, I'm not stopping you. / You know where we are. You're the

MARLENE. Ta ever so.

JOYCE. one went away, not me. I'm right here where I was.

And will be a few years yet I shouldn't wonder.

MARLENE. All right. All right.

JOYCE *gives* MARLENE *a cup of tea.*

JOYCE. Tea.

MARLENE. Sugar?

JOYCE *passes* MARLENE *the sugar.*

It's very quiet down here.

JOYCE. I expect you'd notice it.

MARLENE. The air smells different too.

JOYCE. That's the scent.

MARLENE. No, I mean walking down the lane.

JOYCE. What sort of air you get in London then?

ANGIE *comes in, wearing the dress. It fits.*

MARLENE. Oh, very pretty. / You do look pretty, Angie.

JOYCE. That fits all right.

MARLENE. Do you like the colour?

ANGIE. Beautiful. Beautiful.

JOYCE. You better take it off, / you'll get it dirty.

ANGIE. I want to wear it. I want to wear it.

MARLENE. It is for wearing after all. You can't just hang it up and look at it.

ANGIE. I love it.

JOYCE. Well if you must you must.

ANGIE. If someone asks me what's my favourite colour I'll tell them it's this. Thank you very much, Aunty Marlene.

MARLENE. You didn't tell your mum you asked me down.

ANGIE. I wanted it to be a surprise.

JOYCE. I'll give you a surprise / one of these days.

ANGIE. I thought you'd like to see her. She hasn't been here since I was nine. People do see their aunts.

MARLENE. Is it that long? Doesn't time fly?

ANGIE. I wanted to.

JOYCE. I'm not cross.

ANGIE. Are you glad?

JOYCE. I smell nicer anyhow, don't I?

KIT *comes in without saying anything, as if she lived there.*

MARLENE. I think it was a good idea, Angie, about time. We are sisters after all. It's a pity to let that go.

JOYCE. This is Kitty, / who lives up the road. This is Angie's Aunty Marlene.

KIT. What's that?

ANGIE. It's a present. Do you like it?

KIT. It's all right. / Are you coming out?*

MARLENE. Hello, Kitty.

ANGIE. *No.

KIT. What's that smell?

ANGIE. It's a present.

KIT. It's horrible. Come on.*

MARLENE. Have a chocolate.

ANGIE. *No, I'm busy.

KIT. Coming out later?

ANGIE. No.

KIT (*to* MARLENE). Hello.

KIT *goes without a chocolate.*

JOYCE. She's a little girl Angie sometimes plays with because she's the only child lives really close. She's like a little sister to her really. Angie's good with little children.

MARLENE. Do you want to work with children, Angie? / Be a teacher or a nursery nurse?

JOYCE. I don't think she's ever thought of it.

MARLENE. What do you want to do?

JOYCE. She hasn't an idea in her head what she wants to do. / Lucky to get anything.

MARLENE. Angie?

JOYCE. She's not clever like you.

Pause.

MARLENE. I'm not clever, just pushy.

JOYCE. True enough.

MARLENE *takes a bottle of whisky out of the bag.*

I don't drink spirits.

ANGIE. You do at Christmas.

JOYCE. It's not Christmas, is it?

ANGIE. It's better than Christmas.

MARLENE. Glasses?

JOYCE. Just a small one then.

MARLENE. Do you want some, Angie?

ANGIE. I can't, can I?

JOYCE. Taste it if you want. You won't like it.

MARLENE. We got drunk together the night your grandfather died.

JOYCE. We did not get drunk.

MARLENE. I got drunk. You were just overcome with grief.

JOYCE. I still keep up the grave with flowers.

MARLENE. Do you really?

JOYCE. Why wouldn't I?

MARLENE. Have you seen Mother?

JOYCE. Of course I've seen Mother.

MARLENE. I mean lately.

JOYCE. Of course I've seen her lately, I go every Thursday.

MARLENE (to ANGIE). Do you remember your grandfather?

ANGIE. He got me out of the bath one night in a towel.

MARLENE. Did he? I don't think he ever gave me a bath. Did he give you a bath, Joyce? He probably got soft in his old age. Did you like him?

ANGIE. Yes of course.

MARLENE. Why?

ANGIE. What?

MARLENE. So what's the news? How's Mrs Paisley? Still going crazily? / And Dorothy. What happened to Dorothy?*

ANGIE. Who's Mrs Paisley?

JOYCE. *She went to Canada.

MARLENE. Did she? What to do?

JOYCE. I don't know. She just went to Canada.

MARLENE. Well / good for her.

ANGIE. Mr Connolly killed his wife.

MARLENE. What, Connolly at Whitegates?

ANGIE. They found her body in the garden. / Under the cabbages.

MARLENE. He was always so proper.

JOYCE. Stuck up git. Connolly. Best lawyer money could buy but he couldn't get out of it. She was carrying on with Matthew.

MARLENE. How old's Matthew then?

JOYCE. Twenty-one. / He's got a motorbike.

MARLENE. I think he's about six.

ANGIE. How can he be six? He's six years older than me. / If he was six I'd be nothing, I'd be just born this minute.

JOYCE. Your aunty knows that, she's just being silly. She means it's so long since she's been here she's forgotten about Matthew.

ANGIE. You were here for my birthday when I was nine. I had a pink cake. Kit was only five then, she was four, she hadn't started school yet. She could read already when she went to school. You remember my birthday? / You remember me?

MARLENE. Yes, I remember the cake.

ANGIE. You remember me?

MARLENE. Yes, I remember you.

ANGIE. And Mum and Dad was there, and Kit was.

MARLENE. Yes, how is your dad? Where is he tonight? Up the pub?

JOYCE. No, he's not here.

MARLENE. I can see he's not here.

JOYCE. He moved out.

MARLENE. What? When did he? / Just recently?*

ANGIE. Didn't you know that? You don't know much.

JOYCE. *No, it must be three years ago. Don't be rude, Angie.

ANGIE. I'm not, am I Aunty? What else don't you know?

JOYCE. You was in America or somewhere. You sent a postcard.

ANGIE. I've got that in my room. It's the Grand Canyon. Do you want to see it? Shall I get it? I can get it for you.

MARLENE. Yes, all right.

ANGIE *goes.*

JOYCE. You could be married with twins for all I know. You must have affairs and break up and I don't need to know about any of that so I don't see what the fuss is about.

MARLENE. What fuss?

ANGIE *comes back with the postcard.*

ANGIE. 'Driving across the states for a new job in L.A. It's a long way but the car goes very fast. It's very hot. Wish you were here. Love from Aunty Marlene.'

JOYCE. Did you make a lot of money?

MARLENE. I spent a lot.

ANGIE. I want to go to America. Will you take me?

JOYCE. She's not going to America, she's been to America, stupid.

ANGIE. She might go again, stupid. It's not something you do once. People who go keep going all the time, back and forth on jets. They go on Concorde and Laker and get jet lag. Will you take me?

MARLENE. I'm not planning a trip.

ANGIE. Will you let me know?

JOYCE. Angie, / you're getting silly.

ANGIE. I want to be American.

JOYCE. It's time you were in bed.

ANGIE. No it's not. / I don't have to go to bed at all tonight.

JOYCE. School in the morning.

ANGIE. I'll wake up.

JOYCE. Come on now, you know how you get.

ANGIE. How do I get? / I don't get anyhow.

JOYCE. Angie.
    Are you staying the night?

MARLENE. Yes, if that's all right. / I'll see you in the morning.

ANGIE. You can have my bed. I'll sleep on the sofa.

JOYCE. You will not, you'll sleep in your bed. / Think I can't

ANGIE. Mum.

JOYCE. see through that? I can just see you going to sleep / with us talking.

ANGIE. I would, I would go to sleep, I'd love that.

JOYCE. I'm going to get cross, Angie.

ANGIE. I want to show her something.

JOYCE. Then bed.

ANGIE. It's a secret.

JOYCE. Then I expect it's in your room so off you go. Give us a shout when you're ready for bed and your aunty'll be up and see you.

ANGIE. Will you?

MARLENE. Yes of course.

ANGIE *goes.*
Silence.

It's cold tonight.

JOYCE. Will you be all right on the sofa? You can / have my bed.

MARLENE. The sofa's fine.

JOYCE. Yes the forecast said rain tonight but it's held off.

MARLENE. I was going to walk down to the estuary but I've left it a bit late. Is it just the same?

JOYCE. They cut down the hedges a few years back. Is that since you were here?

MARLENE. But it's not changed down the end, all the mud? And the reeds? We used to pick them when they were bigger than us. Are there still lapwings?

JOYCE. You get strangers walking there on a Sunday. I expect they're looking at the mud and the lapwings, yes.

MARLENE. You could have left.

JOYCE. Who says I wanted to leave?

MARLENE. Stop getting at me then, you're really boring.

JOYCE. How could I have left?

MARLENE. Did you want to?

JOYCE. I said how, / how could I?

MARLENE. If you'd wanted to you'd have done it.

JOYCE. Christ.

MARLENE. Are we getting drunk?

JOYCE. Do you want something to eat?

MARLENE. No, I'm getting drunk.

JOYCE. Funny time to visit, Sunday evening.

MARLENE. I came this morning. I spent the day.

ANGIE (off). Aunty! Aunty Marlene!

MARLENE. I'd better go.

JOYCE. Go on then.

MARLENE. All right.

ANGIE (off). Aunty! Can you hear me? I'm ready.

> MARLENE goes.
>
> JOYCE goes on sitting.
>
> MARLENE comes back.

JOYCE. So what's the secret?

MARLENE. It's a secret.

JOYCE. I know what it is anyway.

MARLENE. I bet you don't. You always said that.

JOYCE. It's her exercise book.

MARLENE. Yes, but you don't know what's in it.

JOYCE. It's some game, some secret society she has with Kit.

MARLENE. You don't know the password. You don't know the code.

JOYCE. You're really in it, aren't you. Can you do the handshake?

MARLENE. She didn't mention a handshake.

JOYCE. I thought they'd have a special handshake. She spends hours writing that but she's useless at school. She copies things out of books about black magic, and politicians out of the paper. It's a bit childish.

MARLENE. I think it's a plot to take over the world.

JOYCE. She's been in the remedial class the last two years.

MARLENE. I came up this morning and spent the day in Ipswich.
   I went to see mother.

JOYCE. Did she recognise you?

MARLENE. Are you trying to be funny?

JOYCE. No, she does wander.

MARLENE. She wasn't wandering at all, she was very lucid thank
   you.

JOYCE. You were very lucky then.

MARLENE. Fucking awful life she's had.

JOYCE. Don't tell me.

MARLENE. Fucking waste.

JOYCE. Don't talk to me.

MARLENE. Why shouldn't I talk? Why shouldn't I talk to you? /
   Isn't she my mother too?

JOYCE. Look, you've left, you've gone away, / we can do
   without you.

MARLENE. I left home, so what, I left home. People do leave
   home / it is normal.

JOYCE. We understand that, we can do without you.

MARLENE. We weren't happy. Were you happy?

JOYCE. Don't come back.

MARLENE. So it's just your mother is it, your child, you never
   wanted me round, / you were jealous of me because I was the

JOYCE. Here we go.

MARLENE. little one and I was clever.

JOYCE. I'm not clever enough for all this psychology / if that's
   what it is.

MARLENE. Why can't I visit my own family / without all this?*

JOYCE. Aah.
   *Just don't go on about Mum's life when you haven't been to
   see her for how many years. / I go and see her every week.*

MARLENE. It's up to me.
   *Then don't go and see her every week.

JOYCE. Somebody has to.

MARLENE. No they don't. / Why do they?

JOYCE. How would I feel if I didn't go?

MARLENE. A lot better.

JOYCE. I hope you feel better.

MARLENE. It's up to me.

JOYCE. You couldn't get out of here fast enough.

MARLENE. Of course I couldn't get out of here fast enough. What was I going to do? Marry a dairyman who'd come home pissed? / Don't you fucking this fucking that fucking bitch

JOYCE. Christ.

MARLENE. fucking tell me what to fucking do fucking.

JOYCE. I don't know how you could leave your own child.

MARLENE. You were quick enough to take her.

JOYCE. What does that mean?

MARLENE. You were quick enough to take her.

JOYCE. Or what? Have her put in a home? Have some stranger / take her would you rather?

MARLENE. You couldn't have one so you took mine.

JOYCE. I didn't know that then.

MARLENE. Like hell, / married three years.

JOYCE. I didn't know that. Plenty of people / take that long.

MARLENE. Well it turned out lucky for you, didn't it?

JOYCE. Turned out all right for you by the look of you. You'd be getting a few less thousand a year.

MARLENE. Not necessarily.

JOYCE. You'd be stuck here / like you said.

MARLENE. I could have taken her with me.

JOYCE. You didn't want to take her with you. It's no good coming back now, Marlene, / and saying —

MARLENE. I know a managing director who's got two children, she breast feeds in the board room, she pays a hundred pounds a week on domestic help alone and she can afford that because she's an extremely high-powered lady earning a great deal of money.

JOYCE. So what's that got to do with you at the age of seventeen?

MARLENE. Just because you were married and had somewhere to live —

JOYCE. You could have lived at home. / Or live with me

MARLENE. Don't be stupid.

JOYCE. and Frank. / You said you weren't keeping it. You

MARLENE. You never suggested.

JOYCE. shouldn't have had it / if you wasn't going to keep it.

MARLENE. Here we go.

JOYCE. You was the most stupid, / for someone so clever you was the most stupid, get yourself pregnant, not go to the doctor, not tell.

MARLENE. You wanted it, you said you were glad, I remember the day, you said I'm glad you never got rid of it, I'll look after it, you said that down by the river. So what are you saying, sunshine, you don't want her?

JOYCE. Course I'm not saying that.

MARLENE. Because I'll take her, / wake her up and pack now.

JOYCE. You wouldn't know how to begin to look after her.

MARLENE. Don't you want her?

JOYCE. Course I do, she's my child.

MARLENE. Then what are you going on about / why did I have her?

JOYCE. You said I got her off you / when you didn't —

MARLENE. I said you were lucky / the way it —

JOYCE. Have a child now if you want one. You're not old.

MARLENE. I might do.

JOYCE. Good.

Pause.

MARLENE. I've been on the pill so long / I'm probably sterile.

JOYCE. Listen when Angie was six months I did get pregnant
and I lost it because I was so tired looking after your fucking
baby / because she cried so much — yes I did tell

MARLENE. You never told me.

JOYCE. you — / and the doctor said if I'd sat down all day with

MARLENE. Well I forgot.

JOYCE. my feet up I'd've kept it / and that's the only chance
I ever had because after that —

MARLENE. I've had two abortions, are you interested? Shall I
tell you about them? Well I won't, it's boring, it wasn't a
problem. I don't like messy talk about blood / and what a bad

JOYCE. If I hadn't had your baby. The doctor said.

MARLENE. time we all had. I don't want a baby. I don't want to
talk about gynaecology.

JOYCE. Then stop trying to get Angie off of me.

MARLENE. I come down here after six years. All night you've
been saying I don't come often enough. If I don't come for
another six years she'll be twenty-one, will that be OK?

JOYCE. That'll be fine, yes, six years would suit me fine.

Pause.

MARLENE. I was afraid of this.
I only came because I thought you wanted . . .
I just want . . .

MARLENE cries.

JOYCE. Don't grizzle, Marlene, for God's sake.
Marly? Come on, pet. Love you really.
Fucking stop it, will you?

MARLENE. No, let me cry. I like it.

They laugh, MARLENE *begins to stop crying.*

I knew I'd cry if I wasn't careful.

JOYCE. Everyone's always crying in this house. Nobody takes any notice.

MARLENE. You've been wonderful looking after Angie.

JOYCE. Don't get carried away.

MARLENE. I can't write letters but I do think of you.

JOYCE. You're getting drunk. I'm going to make some tea.

MARLENE. Love you.

JOYCE *gets up to make tea.*

JOYCE. I can see why you'd want to leave. It's a dump here.

MARLENE. So what's this about you and Frank?

JOYCE. He was always carrying on, wasn't he? And if I wanted to go out in the evening he'd go mad, even if it was nothing, a class, I was going to go to an evening class. So he had this girlfriend, only twenty-two poor cow, and I said go on, off you go, hoppit. I don't think he even likes her.

MARLENE. So what about money?

JOYCE. I've always said I don't want your money.

MARLENE. No, does he send you money?

JOYCE. I've got four different cleaning jobs. Adds up. There's not a lot round here.

MARLENE. Does Angie miss him?

JOYCE. She doesn't say.

MARLENE. Does she see him?

JOYCE. He was never that fond of her to be honest.

MARLENE. He tried to kiss me once. When you were engaged.

JOYCE. Did you fancy him?

MARLENE. No, he looked like a fish.

JOYCE. He was lovely then.

MARLENE. Ugh.

JOYCE. Well I fancied him. For about three years.

MARLENE. Have you got someone else?

JOYCE. There's not a lot round here. Mind you, the minute you're on your own, you'd be amazed how your friends' husbands drop by. I'd sooner do without.

MARLENE. I don't see why you couldn't take my money.

JOYCE. I do, so don't bother about it.

MARLENE. Only got to ask.

JOYCE. So what about you? Good job?

MARLENE. Good for a laugh. / Got back from the US of A a bit

JOYCE. Good for more than a laugh I should think.

MARLENE. wiped out and slotted into this speedy employment agency and still there.

JOYCE. You can always find yourself work then.

MARLENE. That's right.

JOYCE. And men?

MARLENE. Oh there's always men.

JOYCE. No one special?

MARLENE. There's fellas who like to be seen with a high-flying lady. Shows they've got something really good in their pants. But they can't take the day to day. They're waiting for me to turn into the little woman. Or maybe I'm just horrible of course.

JOYCE. Who needs them?

MARLENE. Who needs them? Well I do. But I need adventures more. So on on into the sunset. I think the eighties are going to be stupendous.

JOYCE. Who for?

MARLENE. For me. / I think I'm going up up up.

JOYCE. Oh for you. Yes, I'm sure they will.

MARLENE. And for the country, come to that. Get the economy

back on its feet and whoosh. She's a tough lady, Maggie. I'd give her a job. / She just needs to hang in there. This country

JOYCE. You voted for them, did you?

MARLENE. needs to stop whining. / Monetarism is not stupid.

JOYCE. Drink your tea and shut up, pet.

MARLENE. It takes time, determination. No more slop. / And

JOYCE. Well I think they're filthy bastards.

MARLENE. who's got to drive it on? First woman prime minister. Terrifico. Aces. Right on. / You must admit. Certainly gets my vote.

JOYCE. What good's first woman if it's her? I suppose you'd have liked Hitler if he was a woman. Ms Hitler. Got a lot done, Hitlerina. / Great adventures.

MARLENE. Bosses still walking on the workers' faces? Still Dadda's little parrot? Haven't you learned to think for yourself? I believe in the individual. Look at me.

JOYCE. I am looking at you.

MARLENE. Come on, Joyce, we're not going to quarrel over politics.

JOYCE. We are though.

MARLENE. Forget I mentioned it. Not a word about the slimy unions will cross my lips.

Pause.

JOYCE. You say Mother had a wasted life.

MARLENE. Yes I do. Married to that bastard.

JOYCE. What sort of life did he have? / Working in the fields like

MARLENE. Violent life?

JOYCE. an animal. / Why wouldn't he want a drink?

MARLENE. Come off it.

JOYCE. You want a drink. He couldn't afford whisky.

MARLENE. I don't want to talk about him.

JOYCE. You started, I was talking about her. She had a rotten life because she had nothing. She went hungry.

MARLENE. She was hungry because he drank the money. / He used to hit her.

JOYCE. It's not all down to him. / Their lives were rubbish. They

MARLENE. She didn't hit him.

JOYCE. were treated like rubbish. He's dead and she'll die soon and what sort of life / did they have?

MARLENE. I saw him one night. I came down.

JOYCE. Do you think I didn't? / They didn't get to America and

MARLENE. I still have dreams.

JOYCE. drive across it in a fast car. / Bad nights, they had bad days.

MARLENE. America, America, you're jealous. / I had to get out,

JOYCE. Jealous?

MARLENE. I knew when I was thirteen, out of their house, out of them, never let that happen to me, / never let him, make my own way, out.

JOYCE. Jealous of what you've done, you're ashamed of me if I came to your office, your smart friends, wouldn't you, I'm ashamed of you, think of nothing but yourself, you've got on, nothing's changed for most people / has it?

MARLENE. I hate the working class / which is what you're going

JOYCE. Yes you do.

MARLENE. to go on about now, it doesn't exist any more, it means lazy and stupid. / I don't like the way they talk. I don't

JOYCE. Come on, now we're getting it.

MARLENE. like beer guts and football vomit and saucy tits / and brothers and sisters —

JOYCE. I spit when I see a Rolls Royce, scratch it with my ring / Mercedes it was.

MARLENE. Oh very mature —

JOYCE. I hate the cows I work for / and their dirty dishes with blanquette of fucking veau.

MARLENE. and I will not be pulled down to their level by a flying picket and I won't be sent to Siberia / or a loony bin

JOYCE. No, you'll be on a yacht, you'll be head of Coca-Cola and you wait, the eighties is going to be stupendous all right because we'll get you lot off our backs —

MARLENE. just because I'm original. And I support Reagan even if he is a lousy movie star because the reds are swarming up his map and I want to be free in a free world —

JOYCE. What? / What?

MARLENE. I know what I mean / by that — not shut up here.

JOYCE. So don't be round here when it happens because if someone's kicking you I'll just laugh.

Silence.

MARLENE. I don't mean anything personal. I don't believe in class. Anyone can do anything if they've got what it takes.

JOYCE. And if they haven't?

MARLENE. If they're stupid or lazy or frightened, I'm not going to help them get a job, why should I?

JOYCE. What about Angie?

MARLENE. What about Angie?

JOYCE. She's stupid, lazy and frightened, so what about her?

MARLENE. You run her down too much. She'll be all right.

JOYCE. I don't expect so, no. I expect her children will say what a wasted life she had. If she has children. Because nothing's changed and it won't with them in.

MARLENE. Them, them. / Us and them?

JOYCE. And you're one of them.

MARLENE. And you're us, wonderful us, and Angie's us / and Mum and Dad's us.

JOYCE. Yes, that's right, and you're them.

MARLENE. Come on, Joyce, what a night. You've got what it takes.

JOYCE. I know I have.

MARLENE. I didn't really mean all that.

JOYCE. I did.

MARLENE. But we're friends anyway.

JOYCE. I don't think so, no.

MARLENE. Well it's lovely to be out in the country. I really must make the effort to come more often.
I want to go to sleep.
I want to go to sleep.

JOYCE gets blankets for the sofa.

JOYCE. Goodnight then. I hope you'll be warm enough.

MARLENE. Goodnight. Joyce —

JOYCE. No, pet. Sorry.

JOYCE goes.

MARLENE sits wrapped in a blanket and has another drink.

ANGIE comes in.

ANGIE. Mum?

MARLENE. Angie? What's the matter?

ANGIE. Mum?

MARLENE. No, she's gone to bed. It's Aunty Marlene.

ANGIE. Frightening.

MARLENE. Did you have a bad dream? What happened in it?
Well you're awake now, aren't you pet?

ANGIE. Frightening.

Notes

Act One

1 *Frascati*: popular Italian dry white wine.

1 *Hawaii*: a group of islands in the Pacific Ocean – the 'ideal' holiday destination – whose capital is Honolulu. Discovered by Captain Cook in 1778, they were originally named the Sandwich Islands. Annexed by the USA in 1898, they became that country's fiftieth state in 1959.

1 *Tobermory*: a small Scottish burgh (i.e. borough) on the north coast of the island of Mull, Argyllshire.

2 *miss its face*: miss seeing her. The use of 'its' is patronising.

2 *sake*: (also saki, or sakki) Japan's chief alcoholic drink, similar to beer but clearer in texture and made from fermented rice.

2 *Let the wild goose come to me this spring*: metaphorical allusion meaning bring her (Nijo) to my bed.

3 *metaphysical poets*: school of English poets of the early seventeenth century whose work is characterised by concision, ingenious, often highly intricate word-play (known as 'conceits') and striking imagery. The best-known exponent was John Donne (1571–1631) whose early love poetry gave way to the writing of religious sonnets when he took holy orders and, later, became Dean of St Paul's in London.

3 *hymnology*: study of the history and composition of religious hymns.

3 *without matter*: without physical substance.

4 *Waldorf salad*: a salad of apple, celery and walnuts.

4 *John the Scot*: John Duns 'Scotus', thirteenth-century philosopher and theologian. His date indicates the extent of Churchill's inventiveness with regard to Pope Joan who didn't really exist.

5 *Canelloni*: Italian pasta dish.

5 *Avocado vinaigrette*: large pear-shaped fruit, usually served in half with a dressing of oil and vinegar.

6 *Buddhism ... in Japan*: the Buddhist religion originated in
India around 500 BC and derives from the teachings of
Buddha whose most important doctrine is that of *karma* –
good or evil deeds reaping an appropriate reward in this life
or (through reincarnation) a succession of lives. The main
divisions are *Theravada* in South-East Asia and *Mahayana* in
North Asia. *Lamaism* in Tibet and *Zen* in Japan are among
the many *Mahayana* sects.

6 *Mahayana sutras*: Buddhistic textbooks.

7 *brace*: refresh, stimulate.

7 *acacias*: one of a large group of shrubs and trees belonging to
the pea family. Acacias include the thorn trees of the African
savannah and the gum Arabic tree of North Africa.

8 *the Sandwich Isles*: see note on *Hawaii* (p. 88). When
Captain Cook named the Pacific islands it was in honour of
Lord Sandwich, who also lent his name to the common
snack.

8 *Lady Betto*: court lady, contemporary of Nijo.

10 *one of the three lower realms*: the lowest of six realms into
which the human spirit can be reborn according to Buddhist
thought.

10 *St Augustine*: St Augustine of Hippo (354–430) (not to be
confused with St Augustine, Archbishop of Canterbury, who
died in 604). Among his many writings are his *Confessions*,
a spiritual autobiography, and *The City of God* which sets
out, in twenty-two books, to vindicate the Christian Church
and Divine Providence.

10 *Neo-Platonic Ideas*: 'Ideal Forms' derived from the Greek
philosopher Plato (426–347 BC), a pupil of Socrates and
teacher of Aristotle. He was the author of philosophical
dialogues on such topics as metaphysics, ethics and politics.
Central to his teaching is the notion of 'Ideal Forms' which
he located outside the everyday world and which, for him,
constituted 'ideal' versions of reality. The nature of these
ideas subsequently lent themselves conveniently to religious
modes of thought. In Neoplatonism, after death all life
returns to its original source where it is stripped of individual
identity, a process called *henosis*. In Orthodox Christianity,
on the other hand, *theosis* gives the individual the possibility

of uniting with God in divine eternal union.

10 *Denys the Areopagite . . . the pseudo-Denys*: pseudo-
   Dionysius the Areopagite (also known as the pseudo-Denys)
   was an anonymous theologian and philosopher of the late
   fifth century. One of his most important works, *Corpus
   Areopagiticus*, was mistakenly attributed to someone of the
   same name who was known as Dionysius the Areopagite, a
   convert to Christianity mentioned in the Bible by St Paul
   (Acts 17:34). The real Denys's works are mystical and show
   a strong Neoplatonic influence. Although the validity of his
   thinking has now been accepted by Catholic theologians,
   many of his claims are known to have been false, such as his
   having witnessed the solar eclipse at Christ's crucifixion and
   of having seen Christ's mother, when he obviously wasn't
   around at the time! An areopagite was a member of the
   Areopagus, an open-air court situated on a hill in Athens in
   Greece, the highest court in the land. It was a site of public
   rhetorical declamation and has become associated,
   historically, with the idea of free speech. The English poet
   John Milton's *Areopagitica*, written in 1644, is an
   impassioned plea for freedom of the press.

11 *carbuncles*: malignant boils on the skin.

11 *erysipelas*: inflammation of the skin.

11 *anaemia*: lack of blood, or of red corpuscles in the blood.

11 *bathchair*: invalid chair on wheels.

11 *gout*: disease characterised by painful inflammation of the
   smaller joints.

12 *Jaeger flannel*: a woven patterned tweed. The trade name
   carries associations of aristocratic taste and expense.

13 *muleteers*: mule-drivers.

13 *offer a horse to Buddha*: a sacrifice, in the hope of a miracle.

14 *chamberlain*: steward.

15 *Theodora of Alexandria*: St Theodora of Alexandria (474–91)
   committed adultery, then, overcome with remorse, disguised
   herself as a man and took holy orders. She was accepted into
   a monastery where she took the name of Theodore. A
   woman who subsequently visited the monastery accused 'him'
   of impregnating her but, instead of defending herself,
   Theodora adopted the child as her own. Her son later

became an abbot. Theodore's true sex was not discovered until her death. Her husband attended her funeral before himself taking holy orders and taking up residence in the monastic cell formerly occupied by his late wife.

16 *Rogation Day*: one of the three days before Ascension Day when litanies of the saints were chanted in procession.

17 *St Peter's to go to St John's*: San Pietro in Vaticano is St Peter's cathedral in the Vatican City, Rome. Considered the mother church of the Catholic community, it is a Renaissance and Baroque edifice built over an earlier structure erected by the Emperor Constantine in 319, over the supposed grave of the apostle Peter. San Giovanni in Laterano (St John's) is the papal bishop's church and is the earliest Roman church building, dating from 313. The only other St John's church in Rome is the Santo Giovanni in Fonte, which stands at the southern end of the Lateran basilica and was also built by Emperor Constantine, who was responsible for bringing Rome within the orbit of the Christian Church.

17 *St Clement's and the Colosseum*: the church of Santo Clemente is known to have existed as early as the third century, although the present building dates from the early twelfth century. The Colosseum (Colosseo) is, as its name suggests, huge – a massive amphitheatre dating from Roman times, much of which remains standing despite fires, earthquakes and looting. It could accommodate over 70,000 spectators to watch gladiatorial contests, animal hunts and even mock naval battles.

17 *Antichrist*: diabolical being opposed to the true Messiah.

18 *bay*: reddish brown.

18 *Rocky Mountains*: a vast mountain range in western Canada and the USA extending from the Yukon to New Mexico.

18 *bronco*: untamed horse.

20 *anorexic*: suffering from an eating disorder that reduces appetite.

20 *Brueghel*: one of a family of Flemish painters, Pieter Brueghel (1515–69) was known as the 'Elder' and is now recognised as one of the greatest artists of his time. Noted for his satirical depiction of everyday life among the peasantry, he was also a wonderful landscape painter, evident in a series of paintings

based on the months of the year of which the most famous is perhaps *Hunters in the Snow*. Some of his last works are considered among his finest, for instance, *Dulle Griet*, a satanic landscape peopled by all the devils of medieval folklore, and *The Triumph of Death*, with its depiction of the almost mechanical destruction of human life, which confirms the permanent influence on his work of Hieronymous Bosch.

20 *Boccaccio*: Giovanni Boccaccio (1313–75) was an Italian poet whose best-known work is *The Decameron*, a hundred tales told by ten young people seeking refuge in the countryside during time of plague. Their bawdiness and exuberance, as well as narrative skill and characterisation, made this work both popular and influential, inspiring, among others, the English poet Geoffrey Chaucer.

20 *Petrarch*: Francisco Petrarca (1304–74) was an Italian poet who, in composing love poems to his divine Laura, popularised the fourteen-line sonnet whose strict form was imported into England by the sixteen-century poets, the Earl of Surrey and Sir Thomas Wyatt. The form was imitated with great success by Sir Philip Sidney and then further modified and anglicised by William Shakespeare in his great cycle of sonnets dedicated to 'Mr W.H. and the Dark Lady'.

20 *Chaucer*: Geoffrey Chaucer (*c*.1340–1400) was an English poet and author of *The Canterbury Tales*, a collection of stories told by a group of pilgrims during the course of a journey to visit the shrine of St Thomas à Becket in Canterbury. He writes in Middle English, the transitional form of the language, which developed from Anglo-Saxon and was close to modern English. Literature at that time was usually written in French, understood by the nobility. By writing in the demotic, Chaucer opened his work to a much wider audience. His other work includes the French-influenced *Romance of the Rose* and an adaptation of Boccaccio's *Troilus and Criseyde*.

20 *profiteroles*: Italian dessert, cream-filled balls of choux pastry covered with chocolate.

20 *Zabaglione*: Italian dessert, egg yolks, sugar and marsala wine whipped together.

27 *Suave, mari magno* ... (Joan's Latin): taken from Lucretius'

De Rerum Natura, II, lines 1–18, 45–7, 52, 55–9. Greg
Giesekam translates as follows:

It's pleasing, when over a swollen sea winds are stirring up
the waters, to watch from the shore another's peril: not
because his troubles are a cause of delight or joy, but
because it's pleasing to recognise what troubles you are
free from yourself. It's just as pleasing to witness battle
being waged across a plain, when you're out of danger
yourself. But nothing is more delightful than to occupy the
calm of an ivory tower built on the teachings of wise men;
from here you can look down on others as they wander
about seeking some path through life, as they strive to be
clever, to out-do each other in reputation, battling night
and day to get to the top of the pile with their power and
wealth. What miserable minds men have! How blind their
hearts are! To waste their brief span of life in darkness, in
peril! Don't they see all nature needs is for life to be lived
without physical pain, while the mind, freed from cares,
enjoys a sense of delight?

27 *We come into hell through a big mouth*: this remark contains
a reference to the medieval mystery plays of fourteenth-
century Europe, some of which were acted out on extended
stages built in front of cathedral buildings, on which the
biblical version of Man's origins and eventual 'fall', his death
and resurrection were enacted against the background of a
number of 'mansions' or permanent settings. The setting for
Paradise was always at the furthest point stage-right while
'Hell's Mouth' was always placed furthest stage-left and was
usually represented by the gaping maw of some monster
which served as both the entry point for those who were
permanently damned as well as an exit point for those saved
at the Day of Judgement.

28 *the Spanish*: Spanish armies invaded and occupied the
Netherlands during the sixteenth century. Their ports were
attacked by Sir Francis Drake. He later commanded the
English forces who defeated the Spanish Armada, which
attempted an invasion of Britain in 1588.

28 *die on a wheel*: a reference to the medieval practice of
torturing people to death tied to a wheel.

29 *Berber sheikhs*: the Berbers are a people of North Africa
   who, since prehistoric times, have inhabited the
   Mediterranean coastlands between Egypt and the Atlantic.
   Their language is spoken by about one-third of Algerians and
   nearly two-thirds of Moroccans. A 'sheikh' would have been
   a Berber leader.

Act Two

30 *Os and As*: 'Ordinary' and 'Advanced' level subject passes in
   the General Certificate of Education taken in British schools
   until 1987, at sixteen and eighteen years of age.
30 *Speeds*: clerical skills, typing and shorthand speeds.
30 *Secretary or typist*: Marlene distinguishes. A secretary usually
   has more responsibility than a typist.
31 *Hundred*: one hundred pounds per week. A decent wage in
   1982 for a twenty-year-old.
32 *a multinational*: a company whose financial interests and
   activities extend beyond the country where it is ostensibly
   based to embrace the globe, with outposts and manufacturing
   sites in several countries often chosen because labour costs
   are cheaper and, therefore, profits greater.
33 *The Exterminator*: the first of two violent films made in 1980
   (the other being *Exterminator 2*), both starring Robert Ginty
   as an avenging veteran of the Vietnam War on the trail of a
   murderous gang and, in Part 2, a mysterious master criminal
   who uses brutal combat skills, learned in the army, to achieve
   his goals.
33 *It's X, innit*: at the time, an 'X' certificate given to a film
   meant that you had to be over eighteen to be allowed in to
   the cinema to see it. The expression 'innit' (a contraction of
   'isn't it?') is an attempt to convey popular vernacular speech.
38 *Your skin's burned right off*: this was an effect of napalm,
   used by the American forces fighting the North Vietnamese
   during the 1960s and 1970s. However, what Kit's reference
   to finding out where they were going 'to drop it' seems to
   infer is the effect of a nuclear attack and the consequences of
   the fireball which occurred when the atomic bomb was first
   used against the civilian population of the Japanese cities of

Hiroshima and Nagaski in 1946. The possible recurrence of an event like this haunted people of Caryl Churchill's generation, especially during the years of the so-called 'Cold War', with the invention of powerful hydrogen weapons and ever more sophisticated means of delivering them.

42 *Third year? Second year*: classes in secondary school covering twelve- to fourteen-year-olds, now termed Year 9 and Year 8.

45 *West Sussex*: affluent area of the Home Counties, close to London.

45 *Marilyn. Esther's Baby. They're all called after birds*: 'birds', a sexist reference to young women, in this case the Hollywood film-star icon, Marilyn Monroe, whose name was synonymous with sexual allure, and, because of the reference to swimming pools, another Hollywood star who was invariably clad in a swimsuit, Esther Williams, who appeared in films with titles such as *Dangerous When Wet* (1953).

46 *Elvis*: Elvis Presley, American singer.

46 *John Conteh*: a Liverpudlian boxer born in 1951 to an Irish mother and Sierra Leonean father. In October 1974, he became the first British boxer for a quarter of a century to win the World Light Heavyweight Championship – a title which he held for four years before quitting the ring in 1980.

46 *pirate*: person or company tempting Nell away from the 'Top Girls' agency with an offer of either more money or better prospects or both.

47 *Prestel*: computerised information service: a large business extension of British Telecom.

47 *IBM*: International Business Machines, a large corporation.

47 *Dymchurch*: a small town in Kent on the edge of Romney Marsh, famous for its light railway which ran via New Romney and Hythe to the lighthouses at Dungeness.

47 *the change*: menopause.

48 *Ovaltine*: bedtime malt-flavoured milky drink.

48 *Ascot*: a small town in Berkshire, near Windsor Great Park, famous for its racecourse, especially the annual Ascot Week patronised by race-going members of the British upper class, where the men traditionally wear morning dress of grey top hat and tails while the ladies wear large, expensive hats and extremely smart dresses. The race is traditionally patronised

by the royal family who are driven down the course in an open carriage.

49 *Pam's ladies*: clients of 'Pam', a colleague of the office women who does not appear onstage.

55 *Madame Tussaud's*: a waxwork museum located in central London. Madame Tussaud (born Anne-Marie Grosholtz, 1760–1850) was a French wax modeller who, in 1802, established an exhibition of wax models of famous people on the Strand thoroughfare in London. This transferred to Baker Street and thence, in 1884, to the Marylebone Road where it remains to this day. Its 'Chamber of Horrors' with wax effigies of famous murderers is especially notorious.

60 *six basic and three commission*: six thousand pounds per year as salary, with three thousand added as a reward for successful selling.

61 *closing on the road*: clinching the deal, completing the sale.

62 *Youngness*: Shona's lack of education is here suggested by her using the wrong word – it should be 'youthfulness' – as well as her redundant repetition of the phrase 'in our family'.

63 *My present job at present*: another example of Shona's use of repetitive phrases. This speech shows the influence of Harold Pinter on Churchill's writing at this stage in her career. Compare, for example, some of Mick's speeches in *The Caretaker* or Lenny's speeches in *The Homecoming*, which contain a similar blend of fantasy and comic pretentiousness.

64 *Who's sitting in my chair? Who's been eating my porridge?*: a reference to the children's story of 'Goldilocks and the Three Bears', in which these questions are asked by Father, Mother and Baby Bear, who return from the forest to find their home occupied by Goldilocks. She has not only been sitting in each of their chairs in turn but has also sampled their porridge and eaten all of Baby Bear's helping. She is then discovered sleeping in Baby Bear's bed but, happily, manages to make good her escape.

64 *I was headhunted*: a reference to the tendency of unscrupulous firms to poach successful, usually commercially aggressive personnel from their business rivals by offering them inducements, financial and other, in order to recruit them. The term derives from warfare among primitive tribes

of cannibals.

65 *CSE*: Certificate of Secondary Education (less prestigious than O level in 1982).

65 *Coca-Cola in Russia and Pepsi-cola in China*: one would expect both brands to be competing in both markets. However, the suggestion here is that, like the oil companies and other large multinationals, capitalist enterprises which are supposed to represent free-market competition in actual fact enter into agreements with each other not to compete but to share, or divide, world markets between themselves, thus maximising the selling price for their particular product.

66 *Violins?*: refers to the musical accompaniment to sad moments in silent films.

66 *Packer in Tesco*: Tesco's the supermarket chain. A packer fills the shelves – a menial task.

Act Three

74 *Grand Canyon*: a vast gorge in Arizona, USA, containing the Colorado River. It is 217 miles long, more than a mile deep in places and between four to eighteen miles wide.

75 *L.A.*: Los Angeles (literally City of the Angels), a port in California famous for its Long Beach and its suburb, Hollywood, the headquarters of the American film industry.

75 *Concorde*: the only successful supersonic airliner, it was capable of flying at twice the speed of sound. The result of Anglo-French cooperation, it made its maiden flight in 1969 before entering commercial service seven years later. However, despite halving the time between Europe and America, the aircraft proved to be uncommerical and, following a serious crash in the year 2000 resulting from design flaws, the aircraft was eventually withdrawn from service in 2003.

75 *Laker*: Sir Freddie Laker (1922–2006) was the founder of Laker Airways in 1966, the first budget airline to offer 'no frills' flights at low cost – a model which has been successfully imitated by other budget airlines since. His company went spectacularly bust in 1982.

75 *jet lag*: a condition of exhaustion and confusion experienced

by long-distance jet travellers as a result of crossing different time zones.

76 *lapwings*: birds of the plover family known both as the green plover and as the peewit (because of its call). It inhabits moorland in Europe and Asia and scratches its nest in the ground.

84 *Maggie*: Margaret Thatcher (see p. xxxviii).

84 *Monetarism*: economic policy distinguished by control of the money supply (see p. xxxviii).

84 *Hitler*: Adolf Hitler (real name Shicklgrueber, 1889–1945), the German dictator of Austrian origin who became Führer (leader) of the German National Socialist (Nazi) Party in 1921 and was elected Chancellor of Germany in 1933. His ideology, based on German Nationalism and anti-Semitism, was set out in his book *Mein Kampf* (My Struggle) written between 1925 and 1927.

84 *the slimy unions*: a contemptuous reference to the Trade Union Movement – organisations of employed workers first formed during the nineteenth century to undertake collective bargaining with employers to try to achieve improved working conditions for their members. The British Labour Party grew out of the Trade Union Movement but the failed General Strike of 1926 showed the extent to which the Labour Party and the trade unions had diverged. Their comparative power and influence after the Second World War increased and strike action brought down the Conservative government of Edward Heath in the early 1970s. The Thatcher administration after 1979 set out to curb their power through government legislation aimed, in particular, at the powerful Miners' Union. The failure of the Miners' Strike in 1984 led to a subsequent decline in trade union influence in Britain's political affairs.

86 *blanquette of fucking veau*: in the language of French *haute cuisine*, a *blanquette de veau* is a dish of white veal in a white sauce, derived from the French word *blanc*, meaning white.

86 *a flying picket*: trade unionists who support strikes at places of work other than their own. This action was made illegal by the Thatcher administration and contributed to the further

weakening of the trade unions. The legislation confined strike action to a particular workplace, banned 'sympathy' strikes and prohibited other workers from rallying at the site of the strike (known as 'secondary picketing'). It also made the particular strike action subject to a secret ballot of members of the local workforce.

86 *sent to Siberia*: sent into exile. In Russia, from the nineteenth century, convicts and political prisoners were often sentenced to hard labour in this remote eastern area of the continent where living conditions were extreme, especially in winter, when temperatures could drop to as low as minus 40 degrees centigrade.

86 *Reagan . . . free world*: Ronald Reagan (1911–2004) was a Hollywood film actor of the 1940s and 1950s who became Govenor of California (1967–75), before being elected fortieth President of the United States and serving two terms (1981–9). After surviving an assassination attempt early in his presidency, he espoused a form of unfettered free-market politics, colloquially known as 'Reaganomics', which found an enthusiastic ally in the person of the then British Prime Minister, Margaret Thatcher.

86 *reds*: communists. Ronald Reagan was a staunch anti-communist and even labelled the Soviet Union an 'evil empire'.

Questions for Further Study

1. To what extent are Churchill's characters 'top girls'?

2. The absence of men from the play is a clear dramatic decision. Explore Churchill's reasons for this.

3. The historical figures in Act One make an initial presentation of the ideas in the play. What are these ideas and discuss their significance to the wider framework of the play?

4. Marlene's success as the 'new boss' is undermined by her failure as a mother. Discuss this suggestion.

5. 'Top Girls belongs in its 1980s past.' Discuss.

6. 'Don't you get angry? I get angry' (Marlene, Act One). Discuss the importance of anger as a motif in the play.

7. Explore Churchill's experiments with speech techniques, including dialogue, with reference to specific examples.

8. 'I don't know who'd have her, mind' (Joyce, Act Two, Scene Two). Explore the theme of ownership within marriage as it appears within the play.

9. Churchill shows an opposition between work and marriage. Discuss the use of characterisation and staging methods, for example the use of various settings, to express this.

10. 'Nobody notices me, I don't expect it' (Louise, Act Two, Scene Three). The question of visibility is of central thematic importance in the play. Discuss Churchill's treatment of this idea.

11. Marlene's confrontation with Mrs Kidd exposes clear tensions between genders in the workplace. Explore Churchill's treatment of these tensions and the significance of Howard Kidd's offstage presence.

12. The movement backwards in time from Angie's appearance

at the employment agency to Marlene's visit to Joyce's house offers the audience new insights into the relationship between Angie and Marlene. Explore this movement and the related themes and ideas.

13. 'How could I have left?' (Joyce, Act Three). Churchill carefully builds towards the confrontation between the sisters in Act Three. Explore how this is achieved throughout the play.

14. Motherhood and the rights and responsibilities of the mother are sensitively handled in Act Three. How does this act enhance Churchill's treatment of the theme elsewhere in the play?

15. Marlene and Joyce offer opposing visions of the available life choices for women in the 1970s and 80s. Is Churchill suggesting any possible solutions? How are we invited to respond to the dilemmas described?

16. 'I believe in the individual. Look at me' (Marlene, Act Three). Examine the politics of self as it is explored by Churchill in the play.

17. 'Oh God, why are we all so miserable?' (Marlene, Act One). Explore the importance of the themes of misery and joy in the play.

18. The desire to escape through travel and exploration of other cultures is a strong thematic element in the play. What is the significance of this idea to Churchill's examination of the opportunities available for women in the late twentieth century?

19. Discuss the use of humour as a strategy to engage the audience and examine the balance between serious and comic in the play.

20. 'The play is original in presenting so many kinds of women and letting them speak for themselves.' To what extent do you agree with this statement? Explore the range of women represented in the play and the extent to which they can still speak to a modern audience.

21. The possibility of change is the most positive aspect of the drama. Explore Churchill's representation of both change and frustration in the play.

22. 'The distinctive quality of the language in the play is its clarity and incisiveness and how sensitive the text is to live performance.' Examine the use of language in the play as a tool to define social status and character.

23. Is *Top Girls* ultimately a gloomy play?

24. 'The structure of *Top Girls* is unsuccessful and the play falls apart.' Discuss.

Methuen Drama Student Editions

Jean Anouilh *Antigone* • John Arden *Serjeant Musgrave's Dance*
Alan Ayckbourn *Confusions* • Aphra Behn *The Rover* • Edward Bond
Lear • *Saved* • Bertolt Brecht *The Caucasian Chalk Circle* • *Fear and
Misery in the Third Reich* • *The Good Person of Szechwan* • *Life of Galileo* •
Mother Courage and her Children • *The Resistible Rise of Arturo Ui* • *The
Threepenny Opera* • Anton Chekhov *The Cherry Orchard* • *The Seagull* •
Three Sisters • *Uncle Vanya* • Caryl Churchill *Serious Money* • *Top Girls*
• Shelagh Delaney *A Taste of Honey* • Euripides *Elektra* • *Medea*•
Dario Fo *Accidental Death of an Anarchist* • Michael Frayn *Copenhagen*
• John Galsworthy *Strife* • Nikolai Gogol *The Government Inspector* •
Robert Holman *Across Oka* • Henrik Ibsen *A Doll's House* • *Ghosts*•
Hedda Gabler • Charlotte Keatley *My Mother Said I Never Should* •
Bernard Kops *Dreams of Anne Frank* • Federico García Lorca *Blood
Wedding* • *Doña Rosita the Spinster* (bilingual edition) •*The House of
Bernarda Alba* • (bilingual edition) • *Yerma* (bilingual edition) • David
Mamet *Glengarry Glen Ross* • *Oleanna* • Patrick Marber *Closer* • John
Marston *Malcontent* • Martin McDonagh *The Lieutenant of Inishmore* •
Joe Orton *Loot* • Luigi Pirandello *Six Characters in Search of an Author*
• Mark Ravenhill *Shopping and F***ing* • Willy Russell *Blood Brothers*
• *Educating Rita* • Sophocles *Antigone* • *Oedipus the King* • Wole
Soyinka *Death and the King's Horseman* • Shelagh Stephenson *The
Memory of Water* • August Strindberg *Miss Julie* • J. M. Synge *The
Playboy of the Western World* • Theatre Workshop *Oh What a Lovely
War* Timberlake Wertenbaker *Our Country's Good* • Arnold Wesker
The Merchant • Oscar Wilde *The Importance of Being Earnest* •
Tennessee Williams *A Streetcar Named Desire* • *The Glass Menagerie*

Methuen Drama Modern Plays

include work by

Edward Albee
Jean Anouilh
John Arden
Margaretta D'Arcy
Peter Barnes
Sebastian Barry
Brendan Behan
Dermot Bolger
Edward Bond
Bertolt Brecht
Howard Brenton
Anthony Burgess
Simon Burke
Jim Cartwright
Caryl Churchill
Complicite
Noël Coward
Lucinda Coxon
Sarah Daniels
Nick Darke
Nick Dear
Shelagh Delaney
David Edgar
David Eldridge
Dario Fo
Michael Frayn
John Godber
Paul Godfrey
David Greig
John Guare
Peter Handke
David Harrower
Jonathan Harvey
Iain Heggie
Declan Hughes
Terry Johnson
Sarah Kane
Charlotte Keatley
Barrie Keeffe

Howard Korder
Robert Lepage
Doug Lucie
Martin McDonagh
John McGrath
Terrence McNally
David Mamet
Patrick Marber
Arthur Miller
Mtwa, Ngema & Simon
Tom Murphy
Phyllis Nagy
Peter Nichols
Sean O'Brien
Joseph O'Connor
Joe Orton
Louise Page
Joe Penhall
Luigi Pirandello
Stephen Poliakoff
Franca Rame
Mark Ravenhill
Philip Ridley
Reginald Rose
Willy Russell
Jean-Paul Sartre
Sam Shepard
Wole Soyinka
Simon Stephens
Shelagh Stephenson
Peter Straughan
C. P. Taylor
Theatre Workshop
Sue Townsend
Judy Upton
Timberlake Wertenbaker
Roy Williams
Snoo Wilson
Victoria Wood

Methuen Drama Contemporary Dramatists
include

John Arden (two volumes)
Arden & D'Arcy
Peter Barnes (three volumes)
Sebastian Barry
Dermot Bolger
Edward Bond (eight volumes)
Howard Brenton
   (two volumes)
Richard Cameron
Jim Cartwright
Caryl Churchill (two volumes)
Sarah Daniels (two volumes)
Nick Darke
David Edgar (three volumes)
David Eldridge
Ben Elton
Dario Fo (two volumes)
Michael Frayn (three volumes)
David Greig
John Godber (four volumes)
Paul Godfrey
John Guare
Lee Hall (two volumes)
Peter Handke
Jonathan Harvey
   (two volumes)
Declan Hughes
Terry Johnson (three volumes)
Sarah Kane
Barrie Keeffe
Bernard-Marie Koltès
   (two volumes)
Franz Xaver Kroetz
David Lan
Bryony Lavery
Deborah Levy
Doug Lucie

David Mamet (four volumes)
Martin McDonagh
Duncan McLean
Anthony Minghella
   (two volumes)
Tom Murphy (six volumes)
Phyllis Nagy
Anthony Neilsen (two volumes)
Philip Osment
Gary Owen
Louise Page
Stewart Parker (two volumes)
Joe Penhall (two volumes)
Stephen Poliakoff
   (three volumes)
David Rabe (two volumes)
Mark Ravenhill (two volumes)
Christina Reid
Philip Ridley
Willy Russell
Eric-Emmanuel Schmitt
Ntozake Shange
Sam Shepard (two volumes)
Wole Soyinka (two volumes)
Simon Stephens (two volumes)
Shelagh Stephenson
David Storey (three volumes)
Sue Townsend
Judy Upton
Michel Vinaver
   (two volumes)
Arnold Wesker (two volumes)
Michael Wilcox
Roy Williams (three volumes)
Snoo Wilson (two volumes)
David Wood (two volumes)
Victoria Wood

Methuen Drama World Classics

include

Jean Anouilh (two volumes)
Brendan Behan
Aphra Behn
Bertolt Brecht (eight volumes)
Büchner
Bulgakov
Calderón
Čapek
Anton Chekhov
Noël Coward (eight volumes)
Feydeau (two volumes)
Eduardo De Filippo
Max Frisch
John Galsworthy
Gogol
Gorky (two volumes)
Harley Granville Barker
  (two volumes)
Victor Hugo
Henrik Ibsen (six volumes)
Jarry

Lorca (three volumes)
Marivaux
Mustapha Matura
David Mercer (two volumes)
Arthur Miller (six volumes)
Molière
Musset
Peter Nichols (two volumes)
Joe Orton
A. W. Pinero
Luigi Pirandello
Terence Rattigan
  (two volumes)
W. Somerset Maugham
  (two volumes)
August Strindberg
  (three volumes)
J. M. Synge
Ramón del Valle-Inclán
Frank Wedekind
Oscar Wilde